The Iconoclast

Interview with Luigi Carniel

The Aiki Dialogues - N. 16

The Iconoclast - Interview with Luigi Carniel

Simone Chierchini - Roberto Granati

Copyright © 2024 The Ran Network

First Edition

Publisher: The Ran Network
https://therannetwork.com
info@therannetwork.com

Cover photo: © Luigi Carniel

Cover and layout design: Simone Chierchini
Editor: Joseph Kennedy

Some of the images utilised in this book were found online. Despite our best efforts, we could not locate the correct copyright holder. No challenge to copyright is intended

No part of this book can be reproduced or used in any form or by any means without prior written permission of the publisher

ISBN: 9798873966103

Imprint: Independently published on Amazon KDP

S. Chierchini - R. Granati

The Iconoclast
Interview with Luigi Carniel

The Ran Network

Contents

Introduction *by Roberto Granati*	7
Heading Towards the Unattainable Ideal	17
The Arrival at Shizuoka	25
Experiencing the Yoseikan Hombu Dojo	33
Minoru Mochizuki, a Big-Hearted Warrior	39
Seeking the Reality of the Technique	51
Maintaining the Level	63
"Koryu Has Fallen in the Wrong Hands"	67
Memories of Yoshio Sugino	75
The Sclerosis in Katori Shinto Ryu	79
Goro Hatakeyama's Figure	87
The Relationship with Hiroo Mochizuki	93
Where Is Aikido Going?	101
The Study of Weapons	113
Let's Talk About Daito Ryu	117
Seifukai's Philosophy	127
The Value of Reishiki Today	133
Gyokushin Ryu Jujutsu, a Lost Art	137
Forging One's Own Blade	141
The Oxymoron Iconoclast / Transmitter of Tradition	147
About Luigi Carniel	158

▶ *Luigi Carniel and Roberto Granati*

Introduction

Roberto Granati

It was 2001 when I contacted Luigi Carniel *sensei*. Almost ten years had passed since, as a little more than a teenager, I undertook the study of *Aiki-jūjutsu*. Like many young boys approaching martial arts for the first time, I had done so motivated by the mere utilitarian need to 'learn to defend myself.' I had been bullied in the past. The choice to join a *jūjutsu dōjō* was not well-considered; it was exclusively due to the fact that it was the discipline practiced by my father, who, as an officer in the Paras in the 1970s, preferred this art for the hand-to-hand training of his soldiers.

I was, therefore, certainly not aware that I had actually come into contact with a school of Daitō Ryū, one of the most fascinating and complex forms of classical bugei. As my knowledge progressed, I gradually became aware of the wonderful discipline I had been fortunate enough to encounter on my life's path. The impact was so strong that not only did I decide to continue my study of this school even after my first teacher left teaching, but years later, I embarked on an academic study of feudal Japan and the samurai. Aware that I had by no means attained the basic knowledge needed to claim that I had adequately mastered a style, let alone teach it well to the youngsters who entrusted themselves to me, I spent a couple of years desperately and incessantly searching for a Master and a practice that could continue my growth in the school that I had chosen in my youthful and somewhat unconscious enthusiasm as my reason for living.

Seminar after seminar, I got to know numerous teachers and styles throughout Europe. Some were good, others not so much, and there were even some real charlatans in *keikogi*. I always felt that something was missing. It was in this state of frustration that a teacher of modern *jūjutsu* from Milan, who had often helped me, gave me the business card of a Swiss Master he had met in Aosta during a training course. *"I have seen many Masters of Daitō Ryū, including Japanese ones, but this is the one who impressed me the most for technical quality. His daitō is truly powerful, the best I have ever seen. Try to contact him."*

It was in this way that I called Carniel *sensei* for the first time, in my then poor French. Without any problem, he answered me in good Italian, inviting me to a *Daitō Ryū Aiki-jūjutsu* seminar that he was going to hold a couple of months later at his *dōjō* in Neuchâtel.

I went with a couple of students and found myself in his old *dōjō* by the lake with 240 square meters of tatami. The eldest among his disciples still remembers it as one of the most beautiful ever seen (Japan included). I was greeted by this distinguished gentleman with a big smile and a courtesy and affability rarely encountered on the *tatami*. His slender appearance and posture, like an old English gentleman from the 19th century, initially left us a little puzzled, as we are often used to rough and muscular teachers who are very physical and brutal.

Our doubts were dispelled as soon as this international seminar began, with students from many nationalities participating. His technique was fluid yet powerful, elegant yet effective, precise, and concrete. Accustomed to a very set didactic methodology of practicing my previous *Daitō Ryū*, I was initially disconcerted to discover how often my action lacked real effectiveness, once the technique was decontextualised from mere form.

The entire first day was devoted to pure application. On the second day, we worked on the refined *'Tai no kata'* after discovering, at my own expense, how often the technique that I considered absolutely applicable had turned out to be ineffective due to an excess of formalism. The next day, I understood the correct way to hand down a kata and how these two 'legs' of the martial construction could not exist without each other. I also realised they should never be confused and mixed up, which, on the contrary, I had always done unconsciously until that moment.

I was astonished, having witnessed for years the continuous and periodic modification of kata in many traditional schools I had studied, when I heard Carniel *sensei* assert that a kata should never change, remaining in fact immutable.

Like an encyclopedia, it must maintain its pure form to help us understand the applied form through a precise understanding of all those details that, when put together, make a technique functional. This truth, respected with religious reference by Carniel *sensei* over the years, became evident when I made the decision to become his disciple.

Always hosted and treated with equal courtesy as his other students from other countries, I was progressively introduced by Carniel *sensei* to the study, always strictly separate, of the other disciplines he taught, such as *Gyokushin Ryū*, *Tenshin Shōden Katori Shintō Ryū*, and *Batto-dō Kotoken Ryū*. In time, I realised how lucky I had been that day in 2001 to receive a very ordinary business card.

As the years went by, I had the honour of being hosted at

sensei's house and fully understood what Mochizuki Minoru sensei expressed in his concept of *uchi-deshi*. This term is normally used to refer to those students resident in the area where the *sensei*'s *hombu-dōjō* is located. By virtue of their proximity, they attend regular lessons on a weekly basis, distinguishing them *de facto* from those outside, or *soto-deshi*. However, as Mochizuki Minoru sensei expressed several times, for him, the true *uchi-deshi* were not so much those who, living in the same city as the *hombu-dōjō*, limited themselves to attending, albeit regularly, the lessons and then comfortably returning home, but those who, living far away, were forced to undergo intense periods of apprenticeship. This way, they lived in contact with the Master and were able to learn from him not only the mere technical teachings but also the no less important notional and anecdotal component.

In this case, Luigi Carniel sensei, who spent regular study periods each year with his Masters in Japan, perfectly embodies this ideal. His profound knowledge of ancient *bugei*, his genuine desire to pass on the inheritance received unchanged from his great Masters, and his vast martial knowledge, which also embraced the forging and polishing part of a *katana* learned in Fukuoka, could not help but slowly infect many of us. As he often said, this ancient knowledge is like a long chain that began centuries ago and is rooted in the very history of the *samurai* class. Its task is to form the next solid links that will allow this legacy to be passed on, unchanged, to subsequent generations.

For a person like me, sensitised by my university education to the valuable contribution that historical knowledge can make to future generations, it became a sort of moral duty to help this great man. He had honoured me with attentions worthy of a son in his task of perpetuating all these legacies of the past. That is why I was happy when, on this path, I began to be joined by several teaching friends who found, like me, in him a guide and a technical and moral reference. The task of those who disseminate history and culture is not to jealously possess knowledge but to make it as accessible as possible to all those who wish to learn.

The years of apprenticeship with him allowed us to increasingly know the man behind the never ostentatious figure of a great teacher. A man who, like his masters, also stands out for his human qualities that are the fruit of a long and full life lived without qualms or regrets. In the moments of pause between training sessions, this life was nevertheless recounted, allowing us to encounter that world of ancient budō, now increasingly dispersed in didactic and martial systems that, in reality, have little to do with the true world of the *samurai*.

His search for tradition and his unwillingness to accept the often fictitious and stereotyped forms that Japanese martial arts constructed for themselves, especially after the Second World War, have sometimes put him in controversy with many representatives of Japanese martial arts. A frankness of speech and honesty of intellect led him to describe himself as an 'iconoclast.' However, this term, if misread, does not do justice to this great man. His being an iconoclast is not linked to a desire to destroy the image of the *bugei*. Instead, like his sensei did during his lifetime, it is about trying to scrape off the posthumous varnish that had settled over time. The goal is to search, with historical research methodology, for the oldest and most authentic forms of these beautiful warrior traditions.

As a historian, I cannot help but view this 'philological' work on the samurai warrior tradition as the embodiment of an objective historical analysis. This approach should serve as the foundation for any serious research of a historical-cultural nature. Quoting the words of a very esteemed and renowned historian, Prof. Duccio Balestracci of the Siena University—one of the greatest experts, researchers, and disseminators of Italian and European medieval history—the task of a historian is to 'arm oneself with a screwdriver.' This is done to dismantle those historical truths handed down to us, which may also be the result of a series of passages of knowledge that have, in fact, institutionalised things that were not originally so.

This does not mean rejecting all inherited knowledge, but rather, it simply means evaluating the sources we have inherited—customs and traditions—with a critical, non-dogmatic eye. The goal is to clearly discern what is original and what is subsequent, if not fake.

This is the methodology that Carniel *sensei* has developed over the years, and with that note of self-mockery that distinguishes and endears him to many, he has termed it 'iconoclastic.' Beginning with a solid inheritance learned directly from some of the last great masters of the martial tradition—often from *Bushi* families—he has passed on this knowledge without allowing himself to modify it. However, he seeks, through study, investigation, and analysis of texts, to uncover the deepest roots of this ancient knowledge.

Availing himself of a scientific research method that combines direct knowledge, sources, and a form of 'experimental archaeology' through the practice in armour of these schools of ancient *budō*, he has successfully 'dismantled,' to use Prof. Balestracci's metaphor, many axioms that we often take for granted in historical disciplines such as *Daitō Ryū* or *Katori Shintō Ryū*. His efforts help us better contextualise these schools in the period in which they developed and were used in the daily struggle between life and death in feudal Japan.

Those who follow Carniel sensei cannot be insensitive to this aspect of the popularisation of the martial arts he teaches. Technical knowledge alone is insufficient to become his disciple. It must never be forgotten that mere theoretical knowledge is not accepted. In the context of the *samurai*, where a non-functional technique meant facing death, these schools must maintain their full and complete capacity for effectiveness and applicability.

This is why he has always emphasised that studying *kōryū* requires superior dedication and an uncommon cultural ability. While, all things considered, there are no specific impediments to accessing this knowledge and beginning a path in these ancient schools, they are, in fact, not for everyone. Our task is to try to elevate individuals who, like that unaware young man who began his journey in *Daitō Ryū* many years ago for mere self-defense purposes, not only grow physically but also elevate them intellectually. We aim to stimulate their curiosity for higher knowledge.

During the years of study and historical research, spent alongside Carniel *sensei*, I frequently read books, writings, and interviews of his old Masters. Often, I found many of those anecdotes that I had heard from his mouth, perhaps over a beer. I realised how essential the role of us disciples is in keeping these memories alive. Yet, as a historian, I am also aware that the saying *'verba volant, scripta manent'* ('spoken words fly away, written words remain') retains all its dramatic relevance.

In a world dominated by the accelerating digital realm, unfortunately, false news, alterations, and mystifications of historical reality can circulate more easily. If a falsehood or forgery is repeated many times and disseminated, it risks becoming institutionalised in the long run, causing serious damage to historical truth. This is why the work of collecting the testimonies of so many great *Budō* masters that *Sensei* Simone Chierchini has been carrying out for some years now, thanks to his high journalistic professionalism, is very important. He inserts himself into the tradition of great interviews and testimonial collections that were the prerogative of other popularisers like Draeger and Pranin.

The possibility of sharing the voice of my *Sensei* and his testimony with many more people than those who attend his seminars contributes to creating new links in that long chain that is the transmission of *bugei*. According to Carniel *sensei*, serious study of ancient *Budō* must be, first and foremost, a conscious cultural and historical commitment.

In this case, collecting in writing the memories of what is undoubtedly one of the last great eyewitnesses of the ancient Japanese Masters of these *kōryū* becomes a fundamental duty toward future generations of scholars of *samurai* traditions.

▶ Luigi Carniel and Roberto Granati

Heading Towards the Unattainable Ideal

"Your professional journey has roots in the realm of scientific research. After earning your engineering diploma and immersing yourself in the aerospace sector, you played a crucial role in significant scientific projects, such as contributing to the creation of the respirators for the Apollo 11 astronauts and overseeing the design of the gyroscope for the renowned German Leopard 2 tank. What initially drew you to science, and what inspired your decision to transition from this field to dedicate yourself to martial arts?"

"You see, my professional career has been marked by very different moments. In my youth, when I did not yet have a concrete vision of the future, I had experiences that were sometimes completely opposite – in practice, an existence lived under the sign of the saying, much used by us: *'twelve professions and thirteen miseries'*... Before commencing my engineering studies, I therefore led a decidedly eventful life. This period of transition, from a life without a clear vision of the future to one where I became aware that there is a reason for which we came into the world, led me to the decision to turn over a new leaf and not limit myself to a mere existence – 'vegetating' without a goal.

Undoubtedly, reading those philosophers who had always

accompanied my cultural growth was fundamental in becoming aware of this new vision of my existence. Thanks to these enlightened thinkers of the past, particularly the Roman emperor-philosopher Marcus Aurelius, I was able to develop an ideal vision of human behaviour to strive for. Certainly, a utopia and as such humanly unattainable, but nevertheless a value to which one can and must strive in order to elevate oneself. It was precisely this great character from the past who had risen to a figure in whom I could recognise myself – a man who had been a statesman, warrior, and philosopher at the same time, without these characteristics being at odds with each other.

"Obviously, this realisation was the fruit of the experiences of a rather rebellious young man, but it was enough to mark the subsequent course of my life. The five years that marked my academic journey up to graduation were intense years of dogged study alongside the work I necessarily had to do to support myself and martial arts training. Reflecting today on that very intense period, I cannot help but make a comparison with the youth of today. In my day, it took willpower, persistence, and sacrifice to keep up with all the commitments I had and to be able to complete my engineering studies. Today, on the other hand, young people complain about too much work and take 'sabbaticals' in order to recharge their physical and mental energies. This makes me think a lot and allows me to become aware of the historical period we are living in as a society.

"When I finished my studies, I had the great opportunity to be immediately employed by a major company dealing with micro-mechanics. I had the enormous good fortune, thanks to this, to participate in the wonderful adventure that was the Apollo 11 project. I was part of the team of engineers tasked with designing the respirators for the astronauts who were to face the first moon landing. To this day, I still remember with vivid emotion the moment when Neil Armstrong and 'Buzz' Aldrin landed, our state of mind

somewhere between excitement and concern: 'Will they be able to breathe there or not?!', we were constantly asking ourselves with apprehension. Despite our calculations and tests carried out on special machines that recreated the conditions of the ultra-vacuum in the laboratory, we were not sure how the materials with which we had built the breathing mechanisms would actually react in sidereal space. Fortunately, we all know how it turned out, and I can proudly say that I participated, as a young engineer, in those pivotal moments in history for all mankind.

"After this exciting interlude, my work gradually shifted towards the design of mechanisms for the armaments industry. In fact, among its many contracts, our engineering office also fulfilled orders for the army, including the gyroscope for the Leopard 2 tank. This mechanism was intended to allow more precise firing of the cannon even with the vehicle in motion. Another task in which I participated was the MATRA Exocet missile. I can discuss this today because the related information has been declassified.

"In this regard, I am reminded of a curious episode that occurred some time ago, prompting reflection on the military secrets in force within the company I worked for. It was during one of my seminars in Belfort, France, around 2012. Among the enthusiastic students who partecipated were a large group of Ukrainians. They had been invited to attend that seminar by my assistant, Roberto Granati, who had previously travelled to Ukraine on my behalf to connect with practitioners interested in joining our organisation, the *Kōryū Budō Seifukai*, and studying our traditional schools.

"During the seminar official dinner, a student of a certain age, who was a respected professor at the University of Lviv, confessed to me that he had known me for a long time. I was puzzled and sincerely told him that I thought this was impossible because I had never been to his country in my life. In response to my statement, he burst into a big laugh and smilingly said, 'The signing of your designs for NASA.'

"Imagine my astonishment when he went on to confide in me that in his youth, he had also been an engineer in Siberia during the communist era, working in the Soviet aerospace agency on armaments and the cosmos. He basically admitted to me that our highly secret engineering work had been cleverly 'flown' eastwards, and he had been able to study it thanks to the KGB. I never thought we would be subjected to such industrial espionage, and I still wonder who could have orchestrated it. Today, I can assert that I am undoubtedly much less naive. This episode made me reflect on how interdependent we all are in the modern world. We believe we are alone on this planet, and instead, we sometimes discover that we are being followed, perhaps from far away, without realising it.

"To return to the initial question – what led me to embrace engineering as a young person – I can assert that it was the thirst for knowledge, the discovery of the technological universe, the chance to improve oneself, the passion for science, and the interest in creating new inventions for the progress of mankind. For someone like me, who wasn't proficient in maths as a child, it was a definite triumph. Surely, it was also a way to make my mother, who suffered a lot during my childhood, happy; let's not forget, I was still a child of war...

"Despite the satisfaction, after years in space and military technology, I questioned the usefulness of it all. Was this really the path I aspired to take? Did I truly want to contribute with my work to the creation of ever more sophisticated devices of death? I honestly realised that this was not what I was aiming for.

"I don't want to sound too pompous by talking about a full crisis of conscience. I prefer to speak of a 'turning point' in my life, a moment where martial arts, which I had always practiced with dedication, acquired more and more space and importance in my daily life. At a certain point, I found

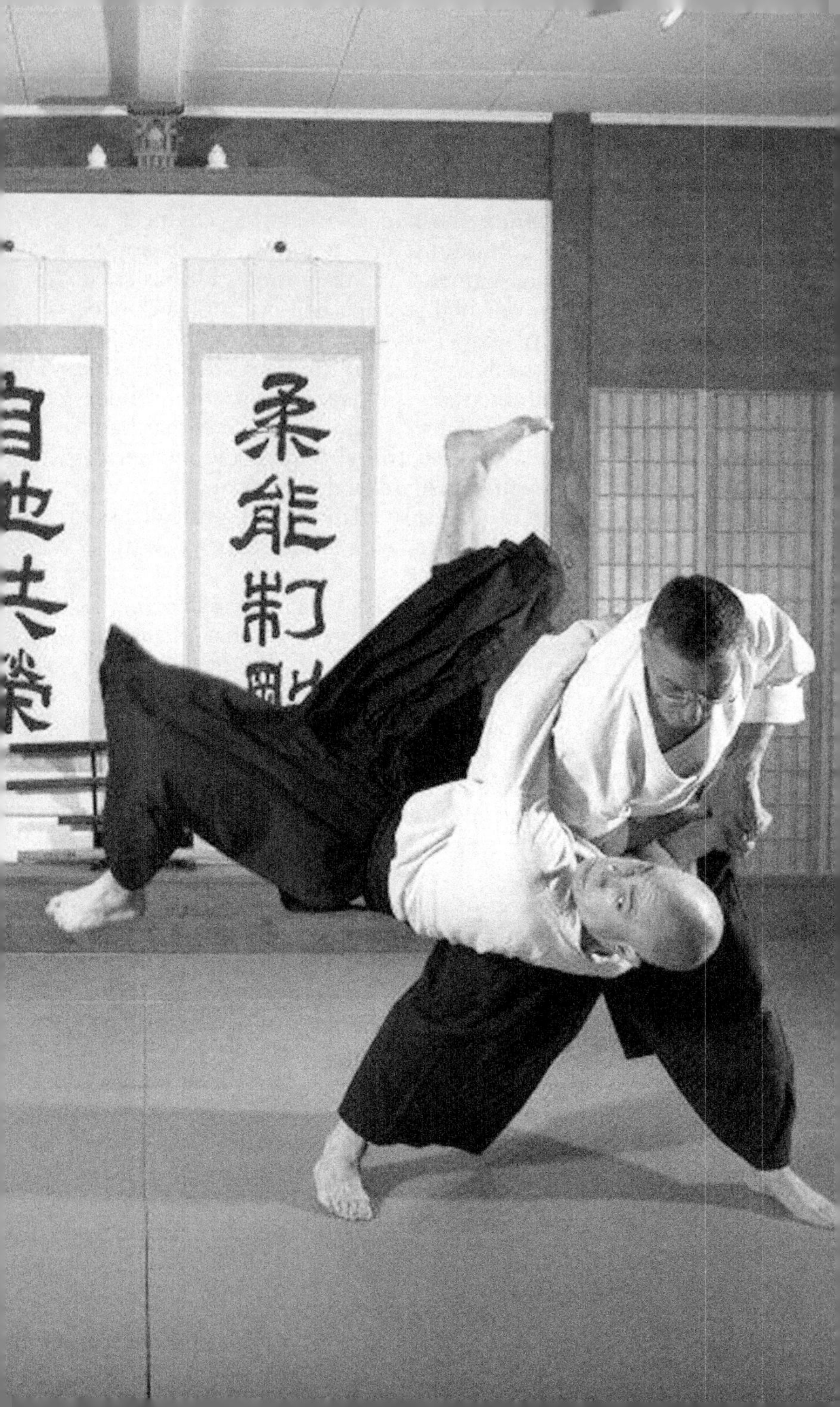
柔能制

myself at a crossroads: either to continue my professional life in the engineering field, which would certainly have guaranteed me a solid future from an economic and social point of view, or to consecrate myself totally to martial arts – to embark on an adventure that certainly offered no guarantee of financial solidity but sincerely fulfilled my ideal of life.

"One could certainly object that such a choice lacked consistency. I was leaving a comfortable profession because it involved designing sophisticated devices of death to embrace martial arts, which are, after all, also a method of taking the lives of other human beings.

"I believe that the reasons behind my choice for the second option were dictated, unconsciously, by the fact that such legacies came from a distant country and culture – a world I had idealised and a moral message I had chosen as my guide. An intellectual richness that I had not found in Western martial arts.

"Martial arts thus assumed the preponderant weight that would characterise the rest of my life. The young man I was then had found in it a Way to follow. Due to my speech impairment, I had unfortunately developed a violent character from an early age. Unable to explain myself with words, I did so with much less 'orthodox' and incisive methods. On this path, martial arts certainly served to channel this difficult aspect of my character and to better manage my problem."

The Arrival at Shizuoka

"In the first half of the 1970s, you decided to go to Japan to drink directly from the source of Aiki, marking the beginning of a series of trips that would last more than 20 years. Typically, such trips by Western students led to Iwama or the Hombu dōjō in Tokyo. What drew you to Minoru Mochizuki sensei's Yoseikan dōjō in Shizuoka?"

"For me to explain what drew me to Japan, it is necessary to go back to the beginnings of my martial experience. I began practicing karate in 1962, at the age of seventeen. Compared to today's standards, where there is a vast array of martial arts training available from an early age, it may seem relatively late, but it was different back then. In addition, Switzerland was lagging far behind the rest of Europe in terms of martial arts offer, especially regarding the discovery and practice of Japanese *Budō*. Only *judo* was predominantly known, while the other Japanese disciplines were perceived as shrouded in an aura of mystery. They were beginning to be talked about, but their diffusion was still in its embryonic state.

"I remember, for example, that my first teacher, Mr Pellegrini from Biel, was a green belt, a level that I, a beginner at the time, yearned to reach one day. In 1964 or

1965, during a seminar in Besançon, France, at the *dōjō* of the Galcier brothers-essential figures of French budō at the time-I attended my first *Wadō-ryū karate* course, and it was there that I met Master Mochizuki Hiroo for the first time. That man impressed me greatly, particularly with the mastery of his *karate* style that I had not previously seen in anyone else.

"It was precisely during that seminar that I had the opportunity to get initiated to the practice of *Yoseikan Hombu Dōjō*'s *Aiki-jūjutsu* because, in that context, Mochizuki Hiroo was also conducting, at the same time, a seminar for this other martial art that I did not know. In fact, the two seminars were taking place simultaneously on two different floors of the building, and *sensei* was commuting between the two halls.

"This was the first meeting I had with Hiroo. In order to continue what I had started with that first seminar, I enrolled at the *dōjō* in Biel where *Yoseikan aikijūjutsu* was practiced under the direction of Mr Hinebnit, who in turn was supervised by Mr Udrisard. We had an enormous hunger for knowledge, and thanks to his regular seminar activities, we began to follow Hiroo wherever he went. I well remember, for example, my first seminar in Paris, his lessons at a *dōjō* in a then decidedly seedy neighbourhood, if I remember correctly, in St. Denis, in the 18th arrondissement.

"I will never forget that first Parisian experience. The lesson began with Hiroo (I call him that because he always insisted that we call him by his first name) introducing us to his local students. Their laconic reply was: 'We are going to turn them into yogurt!'

"At first, we were stunned, and I won't hide the fact that, looking at each other (I was not the only Swiss), there was a temptation to leave without a fight. Instead, we decided not to back down, and I must say that we were right: so much so that there were two injuries on the French side, one of which was caused by me: a very aggressive *ashi-kake* against the calf

▶ Hiroo Mochizuki

of the Parisian student, which forced him to leave the mat. This incident was in addition to a second injury, where another participant had to leave with a sternum that had turned blue (as recalled by one of my companions). In the Swiss group, on the other hand, we were all unharmed!

"This was followed by many other courses, also in Switzerland, with a particular focus on *Aikijūjutsu*. In accordance with our interest in following Hiroo, we decided to create the Swiss federation *"Aikidō Mochizuki,"* later renamed (although we still didn't really know what it meant) to *"Budō Yoseikan,"* where the other disciplines of the *Yoseikan Hombu Dōjō* were integrated into the teaching. It was during this period that we developed a vision of the richness of the martial arts practiced at the headquarters.

"It was only much later, in the early 1970s, that Hiroo wanted to unite the disciplines he taught under a single name, *Yoseikan Budō*. The idea did not initially seem wrong to us; that is, to group the martial traditions imported from the Hombu Dōjō under the same art. Initially, the study of the different disciplines was carried out separately, but soon Hiroo mixed all this knowledge by adding other technical contributions. His aim, as he claimed at the time, was to enrich their efficiency.

"This marked the genesis of a new martial art, the current *Yoseikan Budō*, which included the addition of the posture of English boxing, the adoption of ground techniques, and, above all, the discovery of the famous 'shockwave,' the usefulness of which I still sincerely wonder about.

"By virtue of these new additions, a new personal style uniquely suited to its creator emerged. This distinction helped him set himself apart from other Japanese teachers in the West, especially potential new 'competitors' who were beginning to appear in Europe. Hiroo Mochizuki became the '*soke*,' the founder of today's *Yoseikan Budō*, a kind of '*sogo budō*,' a syncretism of different martial arts.

"In my personal reflections on this shift, it appeared to be a response to other Japanese teachers arriving, along with other Oriental disciplines like *Viet Vo Dao*. It seemed like Hiroo wanted to assert that his style remained the best and at the forefront. These considerations marked the beginning of my disagreements with Hiroo regarding the direction *Yoseikan Budō* was taking in the mid-seventies. However, out of personal integrity, I choose not to disclose the details of these disagreements on these pages. Consequently, in the mid-seventies, I decided to separate from his organization, where I held the positions of Vice-President and President of the Swiss branch.

"It was after this separation that I pondered on how I had arrived at such a decision. I acknowledged to myself that in my uncritical fascination with all things Japanese, I had lost a healthy sense of criticism and analysis. I felt as if, in a way, I had been deceived. Perhaps my pragmatic attitude towards that idolatry without discernment, towards the myth of Japanese tradition—earning me the label of an 'iconoclast'— dates back to that time. And it was in this context that I made my first trip to Japan, to the *Yoseikan hombu dōjō* in Shizuoka.

"In that context, I truly discovered authentic Japanese culture by staying in the home of a SENSEI, living daily in contact with the Master, his wife, and his students. The idea of going to the 'cradle of *Aikidō*,' to Iwama or Tōkyō, never crossed my mind. I immediately felt at ease in the heart of Mochizuki Minoru sensei's home. Perhaps this desire to never again leave the Mochizuki family stemmed from the perception that, despite everything, I found in it that spark of warrior strength that resonated with me."

▶ Minoru Mochizuki

▶ Minoru Mochizuki

Experiencing the Yoseikan Hombu Dojo

"According to Mochizuki Minoru sensei, the term 'uchideshi' did not refer to those who lived in the same city where the dōjō was located, but rather to those who, living hundreds or even thousands of kilometres away, were obliged to live with the master. This made a distinction from the normal student who puts away his keikogi at the end of the lesson and returns home. You had the opportunity to experience this condition for a long time, living during your periods of study with Mochizuki sensei. Could you share your experience as an uchideshi of Mochizuki sensei? How does Luigi Carniel remember this period of his life today?"

"My stays at *Yoseikan Hombu dōjō* were privileged moments of unforgettable technical but, above all, human enrichment. Such an experience marks and conditions you for your whole life. The first things I understood at *Hombu dōjō* were the rigour and seriousness of training without, however, falling into the risk of taking oneself too seriously. By this, I mean that there one avoided that deplorable attitude of superiority that more experienced practitioners often assume towards the less experienced students, so common in many *dōjō*. The duty of a *sempai* is to advance *kohai*, in that spirit of mutual aid and shared growth based on modesty, which is summed up in the motto '*JITA KYO EI*'. It was precisely this feeling of modesty that shone through the figure of *Sensei* as he generously dispensed his immense knowledge. Like a father does with his children, while maintaining rigour and discipline, he encouraged his students to continue to progress without ever belittling them.

"This was totally different from what I had known in Europe up to that point, where teachers, whether Western or Japanese, displayed a latent form of arrogance in their teaching: that contemptuous, condescending attitude typical of those who claim to be the sole holders of knowledge, which they use to guide their unsuspecting disciples towards esoteric secrets of which they alone boast to be the repositories. How much foolishness lies behind this attitude. It was in the presence of Mochizuki Minoru *sensei* that I was able to see and understand what a true warrior was like—a man who encompasses infinite knowledge but, at the same time, exhibits simple behaviour.

"The daily life of an *uchideshi* consisted of a whole series of activities: cleaning the *dōjō* daily, maintaining one's room and the common areas; morning training, focusing on repeating the techniques studied in the previous evenings so that *Sensei* would be proud of us when we demonstrated the results in the late afternoon; coordinating with fellow students to manage food for the day, taking turns buying food for ourselves and for *Sensei* and his wife; and so on.

"In the early afternoon, each of us had the freedom to manage our own schedules, but we all had to be on the tatami by 6 pm for training, which generally ended between 9.30 and 10. Returning to the concept of modesty that should guide a practitioner, it's noteworthy that at the end of each lesson, without exception, everyone offered to clean the *tatami*. No one would ever think of skipping this, and, on the contrary, it became an additional moment of brotherhood among us. We exchanged all kinds of jokes,

including fraternal teasing about some potentially poorly executed immobilisation technique during training, or poking fun at those who, while sweeping the *tatami*, accidentally cleaned their neighbour's feet instead of the mat. Most times everything was shared, including drinks that we might buy and then enjoy together on the *tatami*, with *Sensei* and his wife joining us.

"This, in essence, was the daily life of an *uchideshi*—be it Swiss, American, Australian, Canadian, Italian, Indian, etc. Students from diverse countries and cultures shared a common desire: to learn from such a prestigious *sensei*. The shared aspiration among us was to demonstrate, through our dedication, how much we could surpass ourselves and honour this great man.

"After spending a considerable amount of time at the *Yoseikan dōjō*, I learned to surpass my personal limits, especially in terms of physical endurance. I grasped the significance of meticulous and repetitive practice in honing techniques. The body, inclined towards inertia, needs to be compelled to align with the mind's will. If the mind is weak, so too will be the body. That's why, during my seminars today, I often stress to students: *'Your posture communicates with me, your hands convey a message. In your stance, I perceive and understand who you are.'*

"As I write these lines, many memories flood back, which I had partially buried in the depths of my mind, allowing me to relive, after so many years, the emotions I experienced in my youth."

▶ Minoru Mochizuki

Minoru Mochizuki, a Big-Hearted Warrior

"A whole volume would not be enough to tell the story of Minoru Mochizuki sensei. However, since the focus of the information on him would be primarily on his incredible technical legacy, it would be fascinating if you could portray him from a human perspective. What was the Mochizuki man like? Could you share some anecdotes that characterise him?"

"Mochizuki Minoru was an individual who appeared rough but concealed an unsuspected and profound humanity. A straightforward character, he disregarded the well-known Japanese formalism when expressing his thoughts. Undoubtedly, this characteristic had its costs, affecting his personal and institutional relationships in the martial arts world throughout his extensive life as a *budōka*. Nevertheless, he was a man who consistently demonstrated the courage to stand by his opinions, even when it could be counterproductive.

"I still remember the famous episode that occurred with the Shizuoka police, which I witnessed, and later received a faithful translation of the verbal exchange. At the time, Sensei owned a scooter that he routinely rode into town. He would hop on this vehicle, put on a helmet, and set off. Admittedly, he drove like a *kamikaze* and certainly committed traffic offences. This provoked the inevitable intervention of the police, who sent a car to the *dōjō*. The officers introduced themselves very ceremoniously (after all, they were in front of a very authoritative and highly respected personality, especially in Shizuoka). After many pleasantries, they expressed to *Sensei* their concerns for his health if an accident were to happen with such an unsafe vehicle as a scooter. To which *Sensei* replied: *'Um, I see! You are asking me to stop driving. That's fine.'*

"The policeman answered, *'You understand, Sensei, given your age, we're afraid you might have an accident, and that would be a shame.'*

"Once the police had left, *Sensei* retorted, *'I still drive well, though!'*

"This was one of *Sensei*'s character traits: blunt and direct. Another side of his humanity that I can testify to is his sincere interest in the students he was with.

"During one of my stays, when I woke up one morning, I walked out of my room, which was at the end of the corridor, thus having to walk past *Sensei*'s flat to go to the bathroom. I had put on my *yukata* but unfortunately had no *obi*; so, I kept my robe closed with my hands. Like every morning, Sensei was sitting outside his flat, already intent on writing. I ran past him, wished him good morning, and went into the bathroom. Once back in my room, after a few moments, I heard a knock on *soji*. A hand opened it; it was *Sensei* who, seeing that I had no *obi*, handed me a sort of cord, saying in French: *'For yukata.'* I thanked him, of course, and realised that this man, for whom I might, after all, have been a mere student, had had a kind thought for me and felt obliged to help me.

"This gesture has remained engraved in my heart forever. Here was a man of war and a diplomat, one of the greatest martial arts masters taking care of one of his students: what a man!

"Nevertheless, *Sensei* could also be stern. One evening

▶ *Minoru Mochizuki and Luigi Carniel*

▶ *Minoru Mochizuki wears the traditional Mongolian costume on the occasion of the visit of emissaries from Manchuo*

when I could not attend class (I had a fever because I had caught a cold), *Sensei* sent one of the students to my room to tell me he wanted to see me. I walked downstairs and went up to him. After he checked my forehead to confirm my fever, convinced that I wasn't making up, he said, *'Go to sleep.'* The next morning, to be on the safe side, I decided to be on the *tatami* with the other students. When he came down from his flat to see what we were working on, he saw me and merely nodded with a laconic *'uh'*.

"He had fought in Manchuria and Mongolia, where he served as the administrator of a province with the title of Vice-Prefect (the Japanese Vice-Prefect held the actual governance of the occupied provinces). I personally witnessed the arrival of Manchurian emissaries at the *dōjō* to pay homage to him, during which occasion he even wore their traditional costume. I am aware that he faced criticism for his nationalism at that time, but in Japan, who wasn't a nationalist in those days?

"I recall we had the opportunity to talk about it, albeit rather superficially. I, however, witnessed the deep respect and gratitude that those old Chinese acquaintances from the days when Sensei governed their province felt for him. They appreciated what he had undertaken in those years to improve the assigned area, including the construction of roads, bridges, etc. Therefore, I am inclined to see the man of goodwill behind it all, the human aspect of his tenure in Manchuria, certainly not the image of the wartime occupier.

"Undoubtedly, the close relationship he forged with the upper ranks of the army by virtue of his position as a *Budōka* surely helped to secure the positions he held. However, this is clearly not enough to accuse him of political activism, an accusation that clashes with the aura of the righteous man that has always distinguished him.

"The whole world was going through a bad patch. One only has to think of the many different dictatorships that emerged in Europe: Mussolini in Italy, Franco in Spain, Salazar in Portugal, and the infamous Hitler in Germany, to name but a few. To return to Japan and Mochizuki *sensei*, I believe that those who later accused him did so without truly knowing the man. Perhaps, for the mere pleasure of causing harm, they tried to tarnish the image of a man loved by all, using the ever-popular method of slander.

"He was first and foremost an honourable man. Why else would the representatives of the *Katori Shintō Ryū* have asked him to marry the heiress of the *soke* so that there would be a male continuation within the school? And why would Ueshiba *sensei* himself have asked him to marry his daughter? Because *Sensei* was simply an honourable man in every sense of the word and for that he was appreciated by all who really knew him.

"There would be a thousand other episodes worth recounting—some positive, others less so. One incident, in particular, involved a newcomer to the *dōjō*, and it pains me a little as it reveals how shallow many Western students can manage to be.

"One afternoon, a young Frenchman arrived to spend some time at the *dōjō*. As a preamble, it is important to know that at the Yoseikan HQ, there was a rule that everyone was entitled to accommodation, i.e., food and lodging. I, being the only one who spoke French, obviously explained the rules to this particular visitor: firstly, the one that required everyone, despite the long journey one might have on one's back, to attend the evening course as soon as they arrived.

"When the time to train arrived, this young man did not show up! We began the lesson and sensei went down to the *dōjō* as usual and met the newcomer. When asked why he was not on the *tatami* training, the Frenchman replied that he could not, as he had forgotten his *keiko-gi*.

"Sensei then turned to me, asking if I had one to lend him. I, annoyed by the newcomer's indolent attitude, replied: '*A samurai does not travel without his sword.*'

"While this dialogue was taking place, the Frenchman made a monumental mistake: he sat on *Sense*'s chair with a

Minoru Mochizuki and Morihei Ueshiba

▶ *Minoru Mochizuki and Kisshomaru Ueshiba*

▶ Minoru Mochizuki

blanket on his lap watching, peacefully, the others train! Impassive, *Sensei* sat in *seiza* on the *tatami* and remained there for the duration of the class. At the end, he got up and left with a strange expression on his face. We cleaned the mat and all went to sleep, just ignoring this newly arrived character.

"The next day, as I passed *Sensei*'s flat, he was writing as usual, but I could see he had a face that didn't promise well. He stopped me and, in Japanese, instructed me to tell the newcomer to leave. I felt quite embarrassed to have to be the bearer of such bad news to the Frenchman, who had come specifically for training. However, it fell on me to inform him that his study period at the *Yoseikan Hombu Dōjō* was over before it even began, and he was no longer welcome. Therefore I tried to pretend that I didn't understand, hoping to avoid this unpleasant task. After a few seconds, *Sensei*, without flinching, translated into my language: *'Tell the Frenchman to leave!'* There, I could no longer pretend not to understand and had to perform this unpleasant task.

"Living those years in *Shizuoka* was basically a collection of experiences, some important, others less so, but nonetheless significant of a different way of life. The story of the bicycle comes to mind as a perfect example of the above.

"It happened at the beginning of my time at the *Yoseikan*. One afternoon, I decided to go downtown and asked if I could borrow the bicycle behind the *dōjō*. I was told that it belonged to *Sensei*'s wife, but that she no longer used it and was therefore available. It looked like the thousands of other Japanese bikes, black with a basket on the back and a small plate. I borrowed it and went downtown.

"Promptly, I discovered the intricacies of cycling in Japan, where the rules differed from those in Europe. Riding on the left side, navigating the pavement, being cautious of fellow cyclists, and respecting pedestrians added to the complexity. Crossing the bridge over the Abekawa, which divided the Mukoshikiji district housing the dōjō from the city centre, presented its own set of challenges as the cyclist path was narrow and intertwined with pedestrian pathways. It became quite an adventure. Upon reaching the city centre, specifically in the district designated as a pedestrian zone, I parked my bicycle in the allotted space just in front of the current Starbucks cafe on Gokufucho dori. Having secured my bike, the sole occupant of that reserved area, I departed without causing any disturbance.

"Upon my return, an unpleasant surprise awaited me: dozens and dozens of identical bicycles occupied the same space. In a state of confusion, I attempted to mentally retrace my entire route from the moment I had parked, recalling every detail, but to no avail. Filled with desperation, considering it was *Sensei*'s wife's bike, I randomly selected one from where I vaguely remembered placing it, hoping it was the correct one. From that day forward, I opted for the bus. I can only hope there were no repercussions later, and I entrusted David Orange, an American residing at the *dōjō* with a good command of Japanese, to handle the situation if any issues arose.

"For me, being an *uchideshi* meant being part of a family. Whenever *Sensei* visited my house in Switzerland, he assumed the role of a grandfather to my children and a father to all of us. One particularly cherished memory is from one of his stays when he spent a day observing Swiss wrestling in a village near Neuchâtel, where I reside. He was impressed because he noticed some similarities between this Swiss wrestling form and Japanese *sumō*.

"Here, in a nutshell, is the man who was Mochizuki Minoru *sensei:* a warrior with a big heart, a committed humanist, and a paternal figure to his students."

▶ *Minoru Mochizuki*

▶ Luigi Carniel

Seeking the Reality of the Technique

"In your seminars, you often emphasise that the primary objective in martial training is to preserve the reality and effectiveness of the technique. This perspective contrasts with the present condition of martial arts, wherein the lack of battlefield trials leads to a continuous shift towards a more pseudo-martial practice. Some even describe it today as a choreographed ballet in Japanese costume. On the other hand, in the realm of sports, MMA presents a disheartening spectacle, showcasing how efficiency can deviate from the moral principles of classical schools. How can we maintain reality in the absence of a practical field to apply it? Additionally, how can we prevent efficiency, when disconnected from morality, from turning martial arts into a repulsive showcase of blood and testosterone?"

"Implicit in the question is the answer itself. We discuss martial arts—the arts of war, combat, techniques of destruction empty-handed or with weapons such as *katana, yari, naginata*, etc. This may make some uncomfortable, but according to Mochizuki Minoru *sensei*, all these factors must be considered; otherwise, as you pointed out, it devolves into a choreographed ballet in Japanese costume.

"With that said, it is unfortunate that contemporary 'pseudo-martial arts' have shifted towards a philosophical and humanistic direction propagated by individuals who lack the slightest understanding of the reality of combat, the meaning of physical suffering, and the obligation to train for acquiring naturalness and efficiency in the face of an assailant.

"There are three aspects that characterise this deviation. The first pertains, for instance, to *Aikidō* as a whole, where attempts have been made to embrace the concept of the art of peace. In this context, the adversary ceases to be such and transforms into a partner whose sole purpose is to assist in the expression of harmonious movements. Effectiveness becomes a foreign concept, and choreography supplants applicability. The question of why it is still referred to as a martial art is not even raised. I respect this perspective, individuals are free to pursue their preferences. However, I advocate for choosing a different designation rather than labelling it a martial art.

"Concerning *Aikidō*, there is another factor that gains significance when scrutinising its practice. Some argue that the harmoniously nonchalant approach, where partners execute marvellous falls, and techniques appear disconcertingly easy, is an attempt to emulate Ueshiba Morihei *sensei* as seen in the later stages of his life. However, what is often overlooked is that Ueshiba *sensei*, being an elderly figure at that point and no longer in the physical prime of his energies, projected a certain almost esoteric image in the techniques he performed. This was a result of the profound respect his students held for him, compelling them to accentuate their role as *uke* in his presence.

"Additionally, as reported by Mochizuki sensei himself, Ueshiba Morihei *sensei*'s son, Kisshomaru, consistently faced health challenges. As a consequence, the practice gradually adjusted, in a sense, to the actual physical limitations of the future head of the school (*dōshu*), relinquishing a certain physicality that was inherent in the earlier *aikijūjutsu*.

"Finally, we encounter that image, which I personally find

▶ Luigi Carniel

▶ Luigi Carniel

rather distasteful, propagated by certain Japanese masters and their respective styles of *Aikidō*, where, by virtue of a purported inner strength, they effortlessly overcome any assailant. Let's be realistic! How can we still propagate such nonsense and expect the world of budō not to descend into ridicule?

"I do not intend to be disrespectful to *aikidōka*. I know many of them and have friendly ties with some. However, even the discerning *aikidōka* themselves, who genuinely love their art, acknowledge the shortcomings in their practice and decry this deviation.

"The second aspect involves what I would term 'the real charlatans.' Throughout my life as a *budōka*, I have encountered such individuals numerous times, and I make no secret of the fact that I have no sympathy for them. Shamelessly deceiving people can be attributed to intellectual dishonesty, a serious matter in itself. These individuals parade around, showcasing their emptiness, proclaiming what they do as the true art of superior, invincible, and, above all, non-violent combat. The masquerade stemming from their inflated egos is objectively repugnant to me.

"However, unsuspecting customers regularly fall into the trap of their deceptive advertisements that promise easy practice. Their pseudo-art, a mishmash of different superficial experiences, is, by necessity, subject to continuous 'work in progress' to replenish asphyxiated programs. In fact, these individuals invade other people's mats, attempting to 'steal' the supposedly 'best' techniques. They don't hesitate to film real masters demonstrating a technique during class. Lacking the humility to step onto the mats to genuinely practice and learn through effort, they believe it's a good idea, given their supposed martial superiority, to 'add to their basket' the knowledge of others. They then rework it and present it as the quintessence of their martial research.

"It would be valuable to understand how we reached this point. Setting aside a social-psychological analysis that might divert us from the current discussion, I believe that this deviation in martial arts is a product of a specific vision of our contemporary world in general.

"The current emphasis on the pacifist and non-violent message, cherished by a particular social elite that envisions an idealised world, has gradually led to the imposition of such a perspective even in contexts like history or popular tales. There is a growing demand to purge them of content considered too violent. The justification for this desire to soften reality, aimed at shielding young children from the trauma of violence and fostering peaceful growth, appears even more contradictory when considering that youngsters often seek refuge in video games and virtual realities where violence is unrestricted and uncensored.

"The typical response to this objection may be that young people can distinguish between reality and fiction. However, fiction often appears more alluring. Consequently, both the young and not-so-young are drawn to certain martial arts images portrayed in films and games, images that do not align with the reality of classical budō. This, coupled with the simultaneous desire to appear, a by-product of mass hedonism, leads individuals to identify with these pseudo-martial systems. They may believe that doing so fulfils their need to adhere to labels such as pacifism and love for one's neighbour. Inadvertently, they become victims of the charlatans mentioned earlier. In a world where 'political correctness' compels conformity, these martial forms are better suited to a singular ideology that promotes mass mediocrity and views any dissent as a form of violence.

"Finally, the third aspect involves modern gladiatorial combat sports, such as MMA. In contrast to the first two aspects analysed earlier, these combat sports—clearly identified as sports and not martial arts—are, in a way, the most realistic. Cheating is not possible; the winner remains on their feet, and the loser is on the ground, knocked out. These sports have their own regulations to prevent fighters

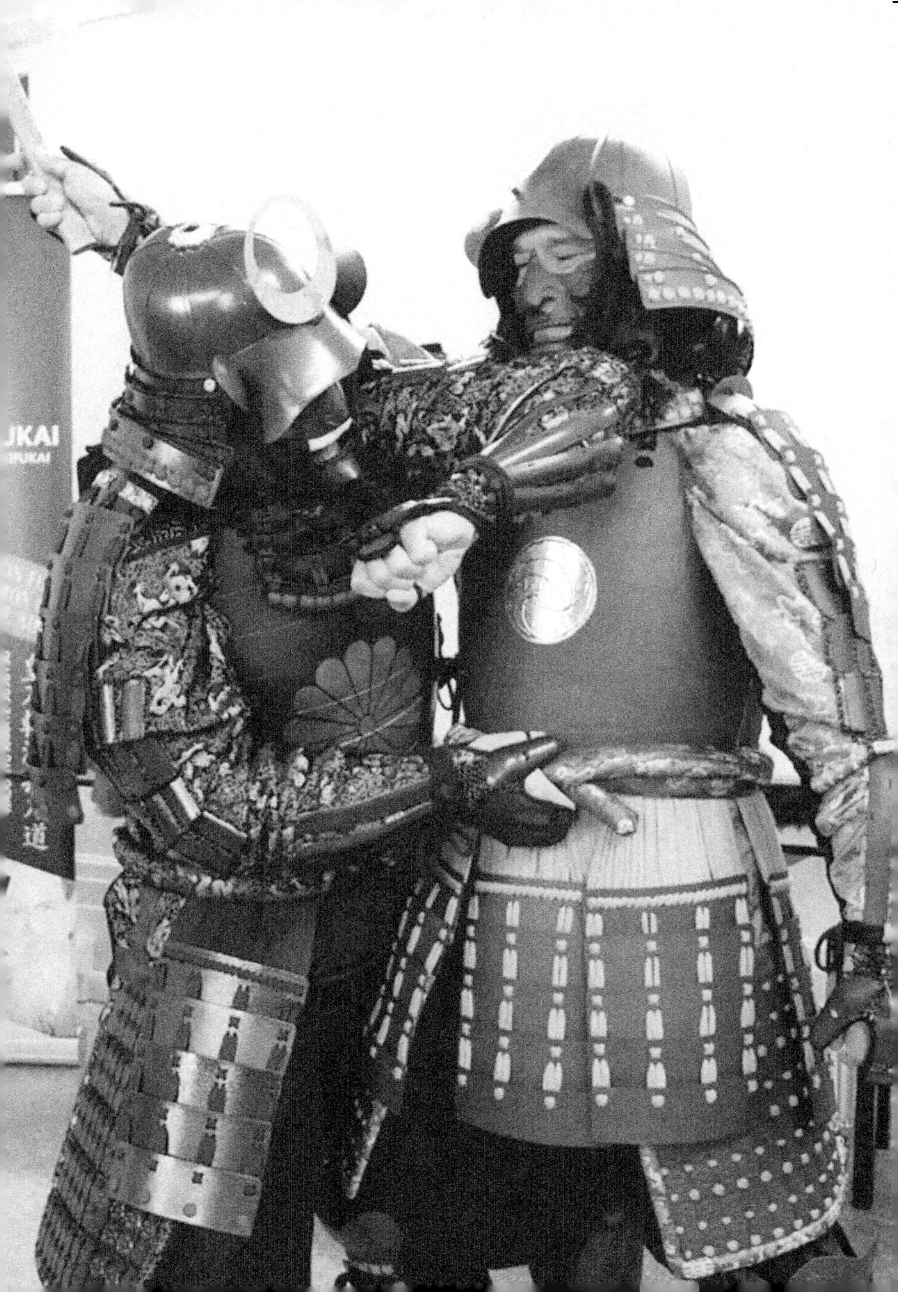

▶ Luigi Carniel and Roberto Granati

from exceeding certain safety limits. Personally, I don't have any objections to it, except for the negative message it sends. For fleeting glory and some money, individuals don't hesitate to harm another human being to prove they are the strongest—for a certain duration. In my view, it's a pitiful spectacle that highlights a desire for pure and gratuitous violence while simultaneously fostering emulation among a certain category of socially vulnerable youth. If these athletes choose to engage in such combat in a ring or a cage, they are free to do so. However, I personally reject the message they convey.

So, how can one practice a martial art that effectively imparts human values worthy of the name—respect, modesty, altruism? In concrete terms, all the martial virtues that elevate a person, while avoiding those that make one vain, gullible, or, worse still, a violent brute devoid of ethics? The practice of a martial art should cultivate being human through the effort dedicated to mastering the technique, focusing on its effectiveness. It involves repeating a gesture thousands of times under various attacks to make it instinctive and efficient, all while avoiding the pitfalls of excessive 'testosterone' and always maintaining a vision of efficiency. The student must acknowledge: *'If my technique is not working, I simply have to work harder! It's not uke's fault for attacking poorly or not following me; it's my fault! I didn't work hard enough!'* In this, teachers play an essential role—they must embody the virtues essential to human fulfilment, much like Mochizuki Minoru *sensei* did.

In Japan, it is asserted that the conduct in the art of war, known as '*Heiho* (兵法),' becomes the same conduct in civilian life, '*Heiho* (平方).' This approach involves being cognisant of the responsibility associated with what we have gained through training and utilising it judiciously, humanely, and with caution.

"My 35 years as an instructor in the Swiss police have made me acutely aware of these principles. Efficiency as a weapon and respect as a duty towards others, even towards criminals. Thanks to their technical proficiency (derived from *Daitō ryū aiki-jūjutsu*), courage, and sense of responsibility, my men have consistently executed missions that were beyond reproach both in terms of humanity and technique. Don't tell me that the old *kōryū* are obsolete and good to be thrown in the rubbish bin!"

▶ *Training Seminar at 186th Italian Paratrooper Division*

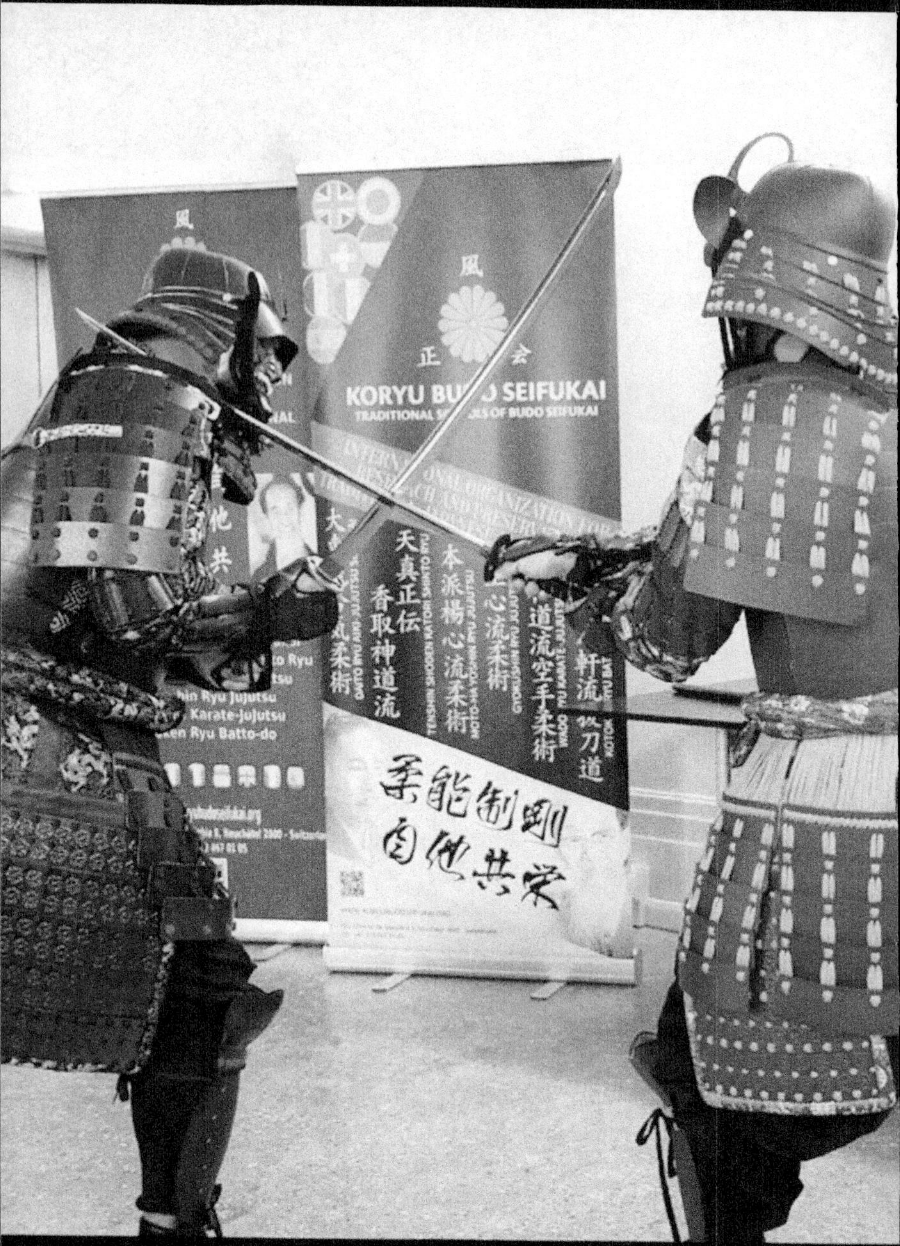
風
正 会
KORYU
SEIFUKAI
天真正伝 香取神道流
本派楊心流柔術
柔能制剛
自他共栄

Maintaining the Level

"You are very careful about awarding grades and diplomas, compared to what is generally done in the European and American jūjutsu worlds. However, your school grants shorter-term diplomas than most Aikidō schools. In your opinion, what are the right criteria for assessing a practitioner's martial arts?"

"Each *dōjō* or organisation has its own criteria based on a scale of values, which the teacher or *ryū-ha* will take into account when granting or not granting a promotion to a higher rank or title. If we speak on a technical level, there is a well-defined syllabus for each dan (scale of values) and the study time required to reach it. This is what I call the common thread, the reference on which teaching must be based to assign an evaluation or grade."

"To give an example, our organisation, the *Kōryū Budō Seifukai*, adheres to a very rigorous programme validated by its members for each discipline. The grading assessments take place during international stages, ensuring complete transparency. If the prerequisites are not met, there is a penalty, not only for the candidate but also, and above all, for their teacher. At *dan* level, the teacher is responsible for presenting a student prepared with the desired requirements, and, justly, is held accountable for this."

"As Mochizuki sensei argued, I start from the assumption

that every student can be a potential future teacher who, in turn, will train other students, thus creating a chain of knowledge that links the past to the present. It is this requirement that keeps the standard at the highest level. If we let our guard down, martial excellence can be quickly eroded, giving way to the spectacle offered by certain pseudo-martial arts observed elsewhere. I am aware of my intransigence, but I believe it is necessary if we want to preserve the true, unaltered historical-technical value of the kōryū arts."

"The criteria for the granting of dan grades, in addition to the technical programme, also derive from the consideration of other parameters: fighting spirit, vigilance, physical presence, perseverance, endurance, etc. These are factors that the examiner, drawing on their experience, must discern and observe in the candidate, yet they are inherently challenging to articulate, being only perceptible.

"What other schools do is difficult to judge because we are not familiar with their criteria; if they are excellent, it is wonderful, and if they are mediocre, sooner or later, they will likely face challenges. Although providing a universal scale of values is challenging, aspiring for excellence and rejecting mediocrity is straightforward. This holds true for *kōryū*; for others, it may not be a priority, and they may not withstand the test of time."

▶ Minoru Mochizuki and Luigi Carniel

▶ Luigi Carniel

Daito Ryu Aiki-JuJu
Tenshin Shoden Kato
Moto-Ha Yoshin
Gyokushin Ryu
Wado Ryu Karate-Ju
Kotoken Ryu Batt

www.koryubudoseiful
Headquarter: Chemin de Maujobia 8, Ne
+41 (0)79 467 0

"Koryu Has Fallen in the Wrong Hands"

"Why do you believe that many kōryū today have adopted features resembling 'historical re-enactment,' placing a strong emphasis on the philosophy and aesthetics of movements, thereby losing a significant portion of the warrior characteristics unique to the period before the Meiji Restoration? To the extent that Mochizuki Minoru sensei often favoured the term 'Bugei' over 'Budō'?"

"I will address this question directly: *Kōryū* has fallen in the wrong hands. Of course, my statement is somewhat of a jest and a provocation. The reality, indeed, is far more intricate than that.

"Let's take a leap back 150 years. Before the Meiji Restoration, all martial arts schools found their *raison d'être* in the existing warrior class. The *Bushi* had to train daily to be prepared for various conflicts that could arise at any time, even during prolonged periods of relative peace. I recommend watching the captivating Japanese film *Rebellion* by Masaki Kobaiashi, depicting the end of the Tokugawa period, to comprehend the conclusion of this era and the associated resignation and weariness of the *samurai*.

"What we now refer to as *Kōryū* were commonplace during this period; each clan had its own school tasked with training the *samurai* of its *Han* on a daily basis. After the Restoration, a significant number of *ryū* had to close due to a lack of students. In order to survive, some opened up to civilians in search of the lost soul of the warrior.

"*Tenshin Shōden Katori Shintō Ryū* is the current and living proof of this shift. In the post-Tokugawa period, courses were initially taught by former instructors with a genuine warrior background. However, over time, the teaching transitioned to civilians who lacked any practical knowledge of combat, gradually deviating from the original purpose for which the school was established. Consequently, *Kōryū*, just like *Aikidō*, transformed into something 'static,' losing the very essence of their practice: the art of war. These new teachers, recognising the interest of contemporary followers in seeking the *samurai* spirit, imparted their knowledge in this new context, without emphasising the arduous journey required to understand all the details of the art. Efficiency was no longer a primary objective, and they no longer had to face the pressure of constant life-threatening situations.

"Add to this decline the impact of the progressive reduction of teaching to the mere reproduction of *kata*. The shift from martiality to some sort of aesthetic philosophy caused the certain decline of *Kōryū*. In fact, the old schools often maintain their art through *kata* as an archaic vestige totally unrelated to combat. It is nothing more than a conventional and indolent series of gestures that has lost all contact with the reality of warfare. This drift is particularly observed in *kōryū* practicing ancient weapons that no one uses anymore.

"It is important for students to understand that a *kata* (a codified form of combat) is a means of learning discipline and not an end in itself. The purpose of *kata* is to understand how to use these weapons on a battlefield. This was the reason Mochizuki Minoru *sensei* resigned as one of the three official representatives of *Tenshin Shōden Katori Shintō Ryū*.

▶ Luigi Carniel

▶ Luigi Carniel

According to him, the school was no longer following the true purposes for which it had been created. Today, we find ourselves in this impasse: how to awaken the warrior spirit in the practice of *Kōryū*, whether armed or unarmed?

"Nowadays, *Kōryū* arts are practised with a completely new spirit, within the current philosophical context. Aesthetics have taken precedence over pragmatism, where detail has become more important than the action itself, and the 'pleonastic' effect is the rule. It is to address these shortcomings that *Kōryū Budō Seifukai* was created with the assistance of, among others, one of my assistants, Mr Roberto Granati.

"Over decades of practice, observing the aforementioned deviations both in martial and ethical aspects, we felt compelled to initiate measures that could counterbalance the inevitable drift towards superficiality and mystification. Like Minoru Mochizuki sensei, I couldn't let this happen without a response. Our objective was to recreate the conditions of warfare in training, encompassing both unarmed techniques and, more crucially, armed disciplines. This involved engaging in experimental archaeology, striving to comprehend and interpret the kata. For instance, *Tenshin Shōden Katori Shintō Ryū* relies solely on *kata*, making us more susceptible to a 'sclerotic' practice and easily becoming confined to the prescribed form.

"Hence, it is our the responsibility of our association to take action, ensuring that we persist in practising and living the kata with passion and sincerity, striving to comprehend their purpose rather than settling for mere child's play. While we may face criticism for our Western perspective (it is a legitimate critique), what is the purpose of endlessly practising something that, in my opinion, would be akin to reciting a soulless *pater noster* or declaiming a heartless poem?

"Minoru Mochizuki *sensei* and Yoshio Sugino *sensei* recognised this issue and manifested their vision by initially establishing the International Martial Arts Federation

(IMAF), which, due to internal problems, was subsequently dissolved. Later, they founded the IFNB, International Federation of Nihon Bugeido, which they controlled.

"Alas! With the passing of these two masters, the IFNB did not endure. Many who were members joined opportunistically, aspiring to one day boast of their association with an organisation created by these esteemed figures, perhaps without fully comprehending its challenges.

"Far be it from us to compare ourselves to these great masters, but something had to be done to curb this shift in practice in some way."

▶ *Yoshio Sugino and Minoru Mochizuki practise Katori Shinto Ryu in the Yoseikan dojo in Shizuoka*

▶ Minoru Mochizuki

▶ *Yoshio Sugino*

Memories of Yoshio Sugino

"*Carniel sensei, you were initiated and studied Tenshin Shōden Katori Shintō Ryū first with Hiroo Mochizuki sensei in Europe and then with Minoru Mochizuki sensei, who then introduced you to Yoshio Sugino sensei, another historical figure in the martial arts of the last century. After so many years, what are your happiest memories of Sugino sensei today?*"

"Ah! What a man! I would call Yoshio Sugino *sensei* a Lord. He exuded nobility and extreme modesty: nobility in his technical and human behaviour, and modesty in the way he taught—always ready to explain what you didn't understand, with his big smile that compensated for the pain and effort needed to learn well and, in this way, make him happy. Like his friend, Minoru Mochizuki *sensei*, both belonged to the older generation; they were still imbued with the warrior spirit, possessing the *Heiho* spirit intrinsically in them.

"I remember once I went to Japan for the Easter holidays and I trained every Tuesday and every weekend in Kawasaki. I usually slept at the *dōjō* on Saturday night; however, on Easter morning, he brought me a tray with breakfast, telling me that he had heard that there was an important holiday (Easter) in Europe and that it should be honoured. How could you not feel obliged to give your all to please this Man who welcomed you like this!

"Sugino *sensei* was a great *budōka* who had also practised *Jūdō* together with Mochizuki *sensei*. One must consider that their masters were none other than the last *samurai* and therefore possessed this warrior spirit themselves.

"His corrections were not focused on the detail but on the why. If my knowledge has developed in this direction, it is thanks to him, who made me see and understand what was important and what was secondary.

"At my place, he would ask me to show him a bit of Switzerland every time because he needed to see green spaces, trees—something that was totally absent in Kawasaki, a suburb of Tōkyō, where he lived. It was there, at his home, in fact, that I first saw plastic trees along the pavements, always green and in bloom. If I may allow myself a comparison between the two characters, Yoshio Sugino *sensei* was a gentleman in the true sense of the word, Minoru Mochizuki *sensei* a warrior with a big heart."

▶ Luigi Carniel with Yoshio Sugino

▶ *Yoshio Sugino*

▶ *Yoshio Sugino*

The Sclerosis in Katori Shinto Ryu

"In teaching Tenshin Shōden Katori Shintō Ryū you have often warned against making this school, like other kōryū, 'sclerotic', inviting your students, when practising, to 'tell a story.' What does this mean?"

"As mentioned earlier, *Kōryū* is often enveloped in a mystical-esoteric aura, conveyed through phraseology taken out of context and, above all, by a total ignorance of Japanese war history. Merely practicing a *Kōryū* is insufficient: one must also take a keen interest in the history and culture surrounding it. Otherwise, we would simply mimic movements without understanding their meaning. Relying solely on what we are told is inadequate, even if it comes from the Japanese themselves. On the contrary, knowledge is acquired through daily practice and personal research—a wise balance between orthodox knowledge and subsequent personal exploration. One must imperatively delve into culture and history while maintaining rigorous practice. Let us not forget that it is through forging that one becomes a blacksmith.

"Regarding *Tenshin Shōden Katori Shintō Ryū*, one of the main causes of its 'sclerosis,' of its immobility, as I mentioned earlier, is its current style of teaching. Presently, this school predominantly focuses on teaching *kata*, and what appears to be the entirety of its legacy is handed down to us Westerners. However, we must not forget that, in this context, the mere repetition of such forms risks confining us to a dead-end box. I consider the learning of *Tenshin Shōden Katori Shintō Ryū* a great opportunity. However, if such practice is limited to copying and merely imitating the so-called fighting forms of the warriors of the past without penetrating their meaning, for me, it is a failure.

"In Japan, in the two *dōjō* named by the *soke*, i.e. Otake's *dōjō* and Sugino's *dōjō*, behind the scenes, would there be things inaccessible to Westerners? This is a possibility that cannot be ruled out, but it seems unlikely to me. According to the mode of teaching I have observed, it seems to me that knowledge is rather limited, not on the syllabus but, in my opinion, in the deep knowledge and interpenetration of this art. It becomes inevitable that the further one moves away from the time when *Katori Shintō Ryū* was a warrior teaching, the more difficult it will be to understand its roots.

"*Kōryū* will then become a beautiful game between two people, where we will correct the insignificant detail: a teaching where, as I happened to notice, weight and credibility are given to the *sensei* who corrects small millimetric details, without realising that he hides a total lack of general knowledge.

"There exists Yoshio Sugino *sensei*'s renowned book on *Tenshin Shōden Katori Shintō Ryū*, of which I had the privilege to acquire a signed copy from the *sensei* himself many years ago. This book was previously translated for a select few, and you can hardly fathom the wealth of knowledge concealed within its pages. It encompasses a comprehensive array of information on technique, the fundamentals of practice, a condensed history, and, most importantly, the book provides an initiation into understanding the terms used to name the kata and their meanings.

"If we take the trouble to understand what *Sensei* is

▶ Luigi Carniel

▶ Luigi Carniel

conveying to us, a door opens allowing us to grasp in depth what we are doing. Yoshio Sugino *sensei*'s work was later officially translated, first into German, then English and Italian. Many practitioners have bought it, but how many have actually read and understood it?

"How do we get out of this impasse? In my opinion, once the learning of *kata* is complete, it is absolutely necessary to break out of the routine of the *kata* itself and also reflect on the way they are named. Understanding and defining the name of the *kata*, for instance, frequently help us interpret it. This, in turn, prompts us to inquire about the reasons behind our partner's chosen positions, contributing to our overall comprehension.

"While this may initially appear obscure and challenging to comprehend, with continuous practice and introspective questioning, we gradually reach a genuine revelation—devoid of mystical or religious connotations, purely intellectual. This represents the ultimate goal of our practice, and without this transformative process, we risk stagnating in a monotonous and tedious routine.

"There is also what I would term the 'theatrical' aspect. I've observed that many Westerners engage in *Tenshin Shōden Katori Shintō Ryū* primarily to don Japanese attire and assert their participation in a martial art. Some may do so without exerting much effort, content to mimic the gestures of a pseudo warrior with a serious and diligent demeanour. I've witnessed outfits reminiscent of Hollywood productions, but it's crucial to remember that 'clothes don't make the man,' and that martial arts practice is open to all.

"*'Tell a story!'*, as I frequently stress to my students. Beyond the learning phase, when gestures become spontaneous and our mind is no longer solely focused on the unfolding *kata*, we should gradually experience a sense of freedom. This allows us to grasp the profound meaning of the action by allowing our intuition and sensitivity to guide us. At this stage in our practice progression, routine dissipates. We come to understand that different *kata* unveil various potentialities within the same movement or attack. Consequently, on a specific movement (or attack), we can adjust and modify our practice according to our needs, fostering a state of constant vigilance. This is the essence of what a *kata* should achieve—telling a genuine story."

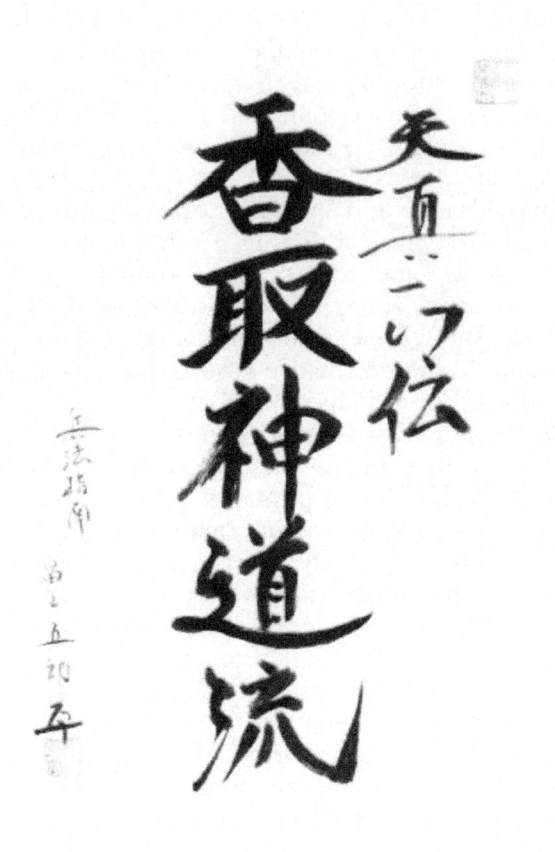

▶ *Tenshin Shōden Katori Shintō Ryū*

▶ Luigi Carniel

▶ Luigi Carniel and
Goro Hatakeyama

Goro Hatakeyama's Figure

"Your martial journey has led you to cross paths with several prominent figures in contemporary martial arts. Could you share insights about Goro Hatakeyama sensei?"

"Another noteworthy figure within *Tenshin Shōden Katori Shintō Ryū* is Goro Hatakeyama *sensei*. Unlike the renowned masters, Hatakeyama *sensei* carried a unique demeanour, never one to assert himself. Despite his unassuming nature, he possessed extensive knowledge of *Tenshin-shō den Katori Shintō-ryū*.

"I had the privilege of knowing him quite intimately. Originating from a humble family, Hatakeyama *sensei* worked as a fishmonger at Yokohama's prominent fish market. As the fifth sibling in a large family, he bore the name '*Goro*.' He resided in the village of Ofuna near Yokohama. Following the passing of his wife, I observed a change in him—some bitterness emerged. Disagreements over his appointment as the 9th *dan* at the Sugino *dōjō* in Kawasaki led to his separation, transforming him into an itinerant master.

"On a personal note, I recall an altruistic individual whose sole concern was the advancement of his students. He imparted his teachings with boundless patience, even when disagreements arose on certain technical matters. However, such differences were cast aside at the conclusion of each session, often over a shared beer and a plate of *gyoza*, a type of Japanese dumpling. Additionally, I remember him as a connoisseur of the good life. During his visits to Switzerland alongside Yoshio Sugino *sensei*, to whom he served as assistant, he indulged in hearty meals and fine drinks without hesitation.

"Following the disagreement he had with the Sugino *dōjō*, we had a frank talk during a seminar held in Gressoney, in the Aosta Valley. During this encounter, I expressed my regret at being unable to continue as his student due to my commitment and loyalty to Sugino *sensei*. In response, Hatakeyama *sensei* wished me the best of luck with a warm smile.

"I am not privy to the reasons behind the internal discord between the Sugino *dōjō* and Hatakeyama *sensei*, although it seemed to centre around the conferral of his ninth *dan*. Regardless, he successfully persuaded many instructors to join him in departure. Among the senior instructors, there was a moment of indecision; some made sincere choices, aligning with either the Sugino *dōjō* or Hatakeyama *sensei*. However, the majority opted for a dual allegiance, a practice colloquially referred to as 'eating at the two shelves' in Switzerland. They believed that by doing so, they could further refine their knowledge of *Katori Shintō Ryū*. When questioned about their indecision, some offered the (perhaps insincere) response that they did not wish to hurt anyone—an opportunistic response. Notably, among them were several well-known teachers. Unfortunately, such is the nature of human beings, or at least, it appears to be the case for some.

"All of this led to a schism within the Sugino *dōjō* community, resulting in endless conflicts that persisted until the passing of Hatakeyama *sensei* due to cancer. Some *dōjō* that had aligned with the *Hatakeyama-ha* were left in a state

▶ *Goro Hatakeyama*

▶ Luigi Carniel and
Goro Hatakeyama

of uncertainty, ultimately having to seek reconciliation with the Sugino *dōjō*. In the interim, the leadership had transitioned to his son, Yukihiro, who, I believe, accepted some but rejected others. It's been reported that those left in uncertainty attempted to seek the validation of their schools from the *Sōke*. However, given the inherent pride in Japanese traditions, a foreign *dojo* will likely never be officially recognised as a mother house, and perhaps rightly so.

"Even the most venerable and esteemed institutions can succumb to human pitfalls, where a thirst for even a modicum of power and opportunism for personal gain can destabilise the entire foundation. I'm not suggesting that such occurrences are exclusive to Japan, but it took the involvement of Westerners for this particular situation to unfold. Nevertheless, I believe that Hatakeyama *sensei* is watching over us from above with benevolence."

► *Hiroo Mochizuki*

The Relationship with Hiroo Mochizuki

"Your association with Hiroo Mochizuki sensei and your involvement in Yoseikan Budo were not devoid of significant events. Hiroo Mochizuki sensei consistently expressed that his inspiration for creating Yoseikan Budo stemmed from the martial spirit of his ancestors and the teachings of his father, Minoru. In crafting this art, he sought to adapt the philosophy, pedagogy, and practices of traditional martial arts to suit the demands of a modern environment and contemporary fighting techniques. Would you like to share any thoughts on this?"

"As mentioned earlier, I can offer firsthand insights into the inception of *Yoseikan Budō*, having been an insider during its early stages. There is much to delve into on this topic, especially for former students like myself who once embraced Hiroo Mochizuki's teachings before his departure, many years ago. I must state that I don't share the same perspective on *Budō*. However, I lack business acumen, and I am not brave enough to weave tales for personal gain.

"Within the *Kōryū Budō Seifukai* today, we have individuals who come from *Yoseikan Budō* and acknowledge its lapse in fundamental principles and the essential depth characteristic of a well-structured school. Yet, they persist in its practice, a phenomenon that remains a mystery to me. This could perhaps be partly explained by the allure exerted by a renowned Japanese master, undoubtedly prestigious, on many practitioners.

"Initially, Hiroo Mochizuki arrived in France alongside Shoji Sugiyama and Jim Alcheik, all three dispatched by Minoru Mochizuki *sensei* to propagate the **budō of Yoseikan** (distinct from *Yoseikan Budō*). Hiroo settled in Paris, Shoji Sugiyama in Turin, and Jim Alcheik passed away in Algeria. Initially, the instruction in the different martial arts was entirely distinct. As his students, we engaged in the practice of three disciplines: *Wadō-ryū karate, Aikijūjutsu,* and *Katori Shintō-ryū*. It is crucial to be intellectually honest and acknowledge the exceptional skill of Hiroo. Rarely have I encountered a martial artist with such speed and competence.

"Towards the end of the 1960s and beginning of the 1970s, the competition from Japanese martial arts masters began to make itself felt. I think that it was then that the idea of creating his own method crossed Hiroo's mind. By establishing his own style, no one could compete with him, as he was the founder, i.e. the *Sōke*.

"I refrain from passing judgement on the reasons that prompted Hiroo to establish *Yoseikan Budō*. What I observe is the evolution this system has undergone over time. Initially, we practiced the three arts separately, but gradually, a heterogeneous blend of fragments from various disciplines emerged, shaping the modern school we are familiar with today. This evolution was further compounded by Hiroo's pursuit of his father towards the end of his life to bring him to France, aiming to strenghten the image of *Yoseikan Budō*. Subsequently, he prohibited

► *Minoru and Hiroo Mochizuki*

▶ Hiroo Mochizuki

all loyal disciples of his father from using the *Yoseikan* name, claiming the role of the designated heir.

"It was in response to this situation that *Seifukai* was established in Japan, a new association founded by Hiroo's brother, Tesuma Mochizuki, with the support of former Japanese and Western students who answered the call to preserve their father's legacy.

"One aspect of this evolution that has caused me considerable distress and continues to evoke deep sadness is the publication of a photo by Hiroo, depicting his father seated in a wheelchair and utterly diminished. To me, this is a genuine disgrace. We should refrain from presenting students, regardless of their identity, with a demeaning image of a master who has served as a symbol for generations of practitioners. Instead, we should uphold the powerful, fiercely warrior-like personality and great humanist that he embodied throughout his life.

"When it comes to traditional philosophy and practice, *Yoseikan Budō* bears no resemblance. The mere fact that the *Yoseikan hombu dōjō* never allowed to practice with music is sufficient to grasp the immense difference! The spirituality we, the old students, experienced in Shizuoka with Mochizuki father was authentic *heiho* and had nothing in common, in terms of atmosphere, with what Hiroo's style has become today.

"What sets *Yoseikan Budō* apart from the *Budō of Yoseikan* is, in fact, primarily the spirit. *Yoseikan Budō* has evolved into a syncretic modern *Budō* tailored for the use and consumption of Westerners. In it, the spirit of competition prevails. In it, it became necessary to shed the 'burden' of the classic warrior spirit, the aforementioned *heiho*, in favour of a 'recreational-sporting' concept suitable for everyone.

"However, the purpose of the *Budō of Yoseikan* is

different – to transmit the true *Kōryū*, maintaining the link between past and present, and above all, to promote the virtues of Man, as previously explained several times.

"According to the information I have received, it appears that there is an effort within *Yoseikan Budō* to revisit its origins, reclaiming some foundational elements that have been neglected for decades.

"Has Hiroo come to the realisation that he may have veered off course? Or is he simply cognisant that his creation has lost its status as an original and trendsetting discipline, compelling him to return to its roots?"

► Hiroo Mochizuki

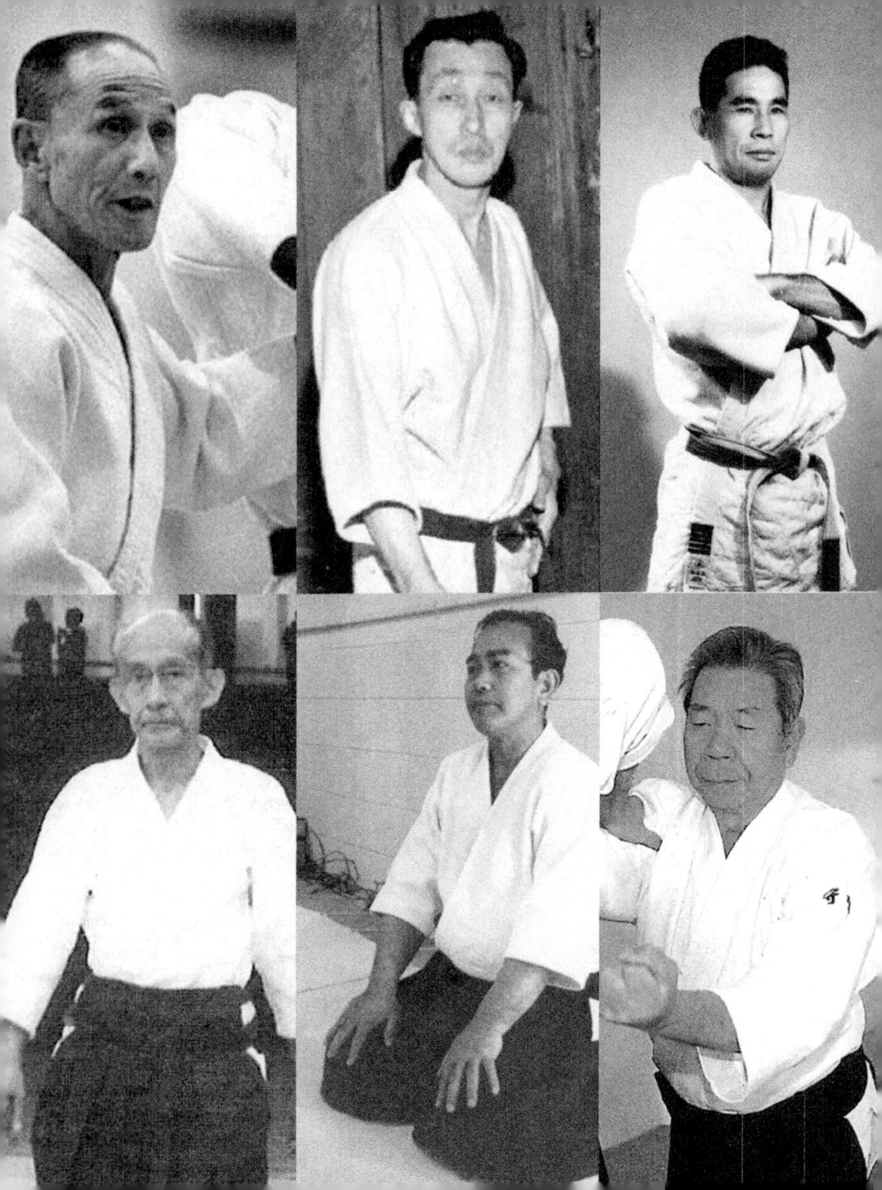

Where Is Aikido Going?

"Aikidō yesterday and today. From the late 1960s until today, you've had the unique privilege of witnessing the evolution of Aikidō. Reflecting on its origins, what nurtured its robust growth, and considering its trajectory for the near future, you stand as an informed observer. Where did Aikidō originate, what environment fostered its flourishing, and what do you foresee in its path ahead?"

"When I began practicing martial arts in 1962, *Jūdō* dominated the scene. *Karate* was often discussed without a clear understanding, and *Aikidō* was commonly perceived as a variation of Judo or something akin to it. Frankly, our understanding was rather vague during those times. In 1964, my introduction to *Aikidō* occurred under the guidance of Hiroo Mochizuki Sensei in Besançon, France. I was there with fellow students for a *Karate* course that he was leading. During this event, he concurrently conducted both *Karate* and *Aikidō* lessons.

"Let's not forget that during that period the nuance between the terms *Aikidō* and A*ikijūjutsu* simply didn't exist. It was only much later, with the arrival of additional Japanese *Aikidō* teachers dispatched by the Aikikai, that a naming controversy arose, ironically initiated by us Europeans. It's crucial to recognise that in Japan, practitioners were not overly concerned with nomenclature. However, we, as Europeans, tended to assume that everyone shared our perspective. It's also good to point out that the founder of *Aikidō*, Sensei Ueshiba Morihei, was one of several teachers that Minoru Mochizuki Sensei followed in his life.

"I believe that *Aikidō* truly flourished due to a more gentle ethos prevailing in the 1960s and 1970s, riding the wave of the pacifist movement propelled by the American Hippie movement, which inevitably influenced the entire world. In my view, it was precisely within this framework that the Aikikai's emphasis on harmony and peace in *Aikidō* practice led people to perceive it as a non-violent martial art. This approach exalted the notion of safeguarding the adversary rather than embracing the conventional concept of physical confrontation.

"In *Aikidō*, the opponent is transformed into a partner who adapts to 'play' their role, creating harmony between attacker and attacked. I must admit that when I observe the movements of *Aikidō*, I cannot help but notice undeniable beauty in them—something not as prominently seen in *Daitō ryū aikijūjutsu*, where immediate effectiveness takes precedence over 'choreography.' This inclination has been further accentuated with the advent of new *Aikidō* styles featuring a pronounced esoteric emphasis. To grasp my perspective, one would need to explore schools such as *Ki Aikidō* and others, which I personally find mystifying in comparison to the original *aiki* message.

"It must be acknowledged that this style of practice has found success among individuals aiming to showcase a martial art devoid of its physical component. They believe that in doing so, they assert an intellectual superiority over those 'brutes' engaging in violence through traditional arts. It's worth noting that some contemporary utopians aspire to banish such violence from every facet of modern society—a notion that is, in my opinion, illusory.

▶ *Il kamiza dell'Aikikai Hombu Dojo*

"In my opinion, after decades of observation, this is generally what *Aikidō* has become. Certainly, there still exists good *Aikidō*—dynamic and demonstrating a certain level of

▶ Luigi Carniel

effectiveness. With the new generation at the *Hombu Dōjō*, especially with the arrival of the great-grandson of the Ueshiba house, there is hope that *Aikidō* can return to its roots as it was in the beginning.

"The majority of practitioners aspire to devote themselves to *Aikidō*, yet often wish to avoid significant physical strain and fatigue. However, this contradicts the essence of Martial Arts, which demands persistent effort, self-discipline, and the sweat of hard work, all for results that are perpetually just out of reach. It bears repeating that martial arts, irrespective of their form, are inherently about dedication, self-improvement without self-satisfaction, and relentless effort. Unfortunately, the modern societal trend tends to transform *Aikidō* into a pastime—a recreation akin to gymnastics for many. Additionally, the increasing ease with which *dan* ranks are granted dilutes the necessary standards."

"For the past few years, what I've humorously referred to as 'harmony-light" has been increasingly prevalent in the mainstream of Aikidō. What are your thoughts on this simplified approach to harmony in practice, which often relies on misinterpreted quotes from Ueshiba and aligns with the postmodern hippie ideology so pervasive in today's official and politically correct Aikidō?"

"Huge debate! I believe *Aikidō* has compromised its essence. It's worth noting that all martial arts, for better or worse, have been commercialised, featured in gyms, embraced by fashion, and portrayed in cinema. This inevitable shift has distanced them from the authentic realm of *Budō*. *Aikidō*'s case is emblematic, as individuals have been so thoroughly influenced that they appear almost indoctrinated in their beliefs. Today, we see practitioners who seem completely detached from reality. Whose fault is it? Certainly not the practitioners, who earnestly believe what they have been told.

"The reason for this can be attributed to a form of 'smoke and mirrors' adeptly orchestrated by the Aikikai itself, which, driven by self-interest, has done little to prevent this detrimental deviation. While it may sound cynical, the motivation can be encapsulated in the adage 'business is business,' a sentiment cherished in the affluent realm of finance. Nevertheless, I don't believe it's the sole cause. I perceive a reflection of today's society, where there is a fervent desire to expel violence entirely—both verbally (through political correctness) and in behaviour. We go to the extent of distorting texts so that our children are shielded from any exposure to violence. Lacking the courage to confront reality, we indulge in 'harmony-light' living, embedded perfectly within *Aikidō*, that present itself as a peaceful martial art. In doing so, practitioners convince themselves of engaging in non-violent *Budō*. However, they overlook the inherent violence within human nature, and even the so-called 'non-violence' is, in reality, a form of violence itself.

"I recently faced criticism from an individual who practices this 'harmony-light.' Our discussion inevitably delved into the perceived violence of the discipline I teach. Amidst the verbal exchange, I noted contradictions in his speech, particularly his reference to what they were doing as a martial art. It dawned on me that the term 'martial art' held no true meaning for this person. Hence, I felt compelled to elucidate the etymology, emphasising its association with 'the art of war.' I suggested, in light of their non-violent approach, they might consider an alternative definition for their practice. This led to a rather spirited diatribe, especially in tone, directed at me. In that moment, I tactfully pointed out, *'Look! Now you are being violent with me. You preach well, but your practice contradicts your preaching.'*

"Violence—the dreaded word that some wish to erase from our minds, under the illusion that we can all lead a harmonious, trouble-free life in an idyllic world where everyone is beautiful and kind. It's clear that such a utopia is beautiful but ultimately unattainable. Life, to some extent, involves an element of violence, and if we understand this well, we can harness it for good. When striving to achieve something, if we don't push ourselves, i.e., apply a certain degree of force to go beyond our limits, we won't be able to realise our potential. It's precisely because of this inherent characteristic of human nature that, by imposing self-

▶ Luigi Carniel and
Roberto Granati

▶ Luigi Carniel

discipline, we can attain our goals. Violence is a part of everyone, and it's up to us to manage and channel it. This is precisely why martial arts exist—to assist us in this endeavour."

"Concerning the point above, I've often heard statements like 'I don't like Daitō-ryū because it is violent. Conversely, studying Katori Shintō Ryū attracts me.' How does the mental disconnect happen, where a warrior school employing a range of weapons with devastating techniques is perceived as 'non-violent' in the collective unconscious of the typical Western martial artist?"

"Yes, I heard that, and in many variations: *'I would like to practise martial arts, but it doesn't have to be violent!'*. *'I am afraid of suffering, of getting hurt, of violent and brutal behaviour'*... *'Yes, I would like to practise but without all that. However, Tenshin-shō den Katori Shintō-ryū seems less dangerous and less violent to me so I can do it'*...

"Once again, this line of thinking mirrors today's society—a leisure society where everything appears easy and achievable in the short term, where effort and duty are discouraged, where politeness is obligatory, and political correctness is a must. Simply engaging in a verbal confrontation can lead to legal consequences. Nevertheless, there is an inherent spark of 'primitive' energy within us, and violence, whether liked or not, is an integral part of it. Humanity has mistakenly equated violence with evil, assigning it a pejorative connotation.

"Returning to the concept of a mental short-circuit, I don't believe people even suspect its existence. They may have witnessed a pleasing demonstration with wooden weapons (presumably non-dangerous), featuring no hand-to-hand combat and hence, no apparent risk of injury. They think, 'Here is an activity where nothing will happen to me,' without realising they are engaging in one of the deadliest martial arts. An incident I encountered during a

Batto-dō (tameshi giri) class serves as an example. Before cutting the *makiwara*, I, as is my custom, provided safety advice to prevent accidents. In my remarks, I emphasised that the *makiwara* should be regarded as a human target: when the sword is still in the air, the person is alive, and once the sword has struck the target, this hypothetical person is considered dead.

"The explanation aimed to convey that, according to the ancient morals of Japanese warriors, effective killing was considered an act of compassion, preventing unnecessary suffering for the opponent. However, one student, when it was his turn to cut, began to tremble increasingly. It became impossible for him to bring down his *katana* on the target because my simple remarks had profoundly shocked him. This incident revealed to me a state of mind in which he was not prepared to confront the real challenges of a martial art. The following week, the student resigned.

"This episode signifies a specific mindset: 'I want to appear but not be.' Consequently, I opt for a martial art that appears non-violent to me, to 'appear,' and reject another where 'being' is a requisite. In essence, this encapsulates what I suspect forms this kind of mental short-circuit: a complete ignorance of the martial context and the notion that a 'harmony-light' in martial arts can be beneficial in life. All of this is, of course, perpetuated by various gurus ready to take advantage of the unsuspecting."

▶ Luigi Carniel

▶ Luigi Carniel

The Study of Weapons

"In numerous traditional martial arts schools, the exploration of weapons was traditionally reserved for individuals who had attained a specific mastery level in bare-hand techniques. In Iwama-ryū, the oral teachings of Morihei Ueshiba emphasise the concept of 'jo ken tai ichi,' which asserts that 'the staff, the sword, and the body are one.' This principle suggests that the study of weapons and empty-hand techniques should occur simultaneously.

"What are your thoughts on this approach, and how does it influence your teaching methodology?"

"Morihei Ueshiba sensei was undoubtedly correct; weapons should constitute an integral part of a warrior's learning process. Yet, in many *dōjō*, the common response to students requesting weapons training is to advise them to wait until they have attained proficiency in bare-hand techniques. This stance often overlooks the historical context of the warrior era. Did it truly take years to prepare for battle in those times? No, training was inherently intensive and all-encompassing. *Samurai* needed to be adept at handling diverse situations after a relatively brief apprenticeship. If I may draw a parallel, I'd liken *samurai* training to that of contemporary special forces in modern armies. Telling a present-day soldier that they can only learn to handle a rifle, machine gun, etc., if they excel in hand-to-hand combat is objectively impractical.

"Any objections? In the realm of *Budō*, there's always a 'but'. I can objectively understand the idea of starting with empty-handed practice. Why does this make historical sense? During the Meiji Restoration, schools fragmented, keeping only what would interest new students. With practitioners no longer strolling the streets fully armed, martial arts schools began focusing on notions essential for self-defense. Consequently, schools retained hand-to-hand combat, and the study of weapons gradually faded.

"On the flip side, examining the *Butokuden* comprehensive treatise on the ancient schools reveals that each school encompassed various teachings: sword practice (*Kenjutsu*), hand-to-hand practice (Jūjutsu), spear practice (*Sōjutsu*), and more.

"All the above considered, the methodology I endorse in my school and within the *Kōryū Budō Seifukai* involves a thorough and comprehensive exploration of the various disciplines at our disposal. This approach entails teaching each discipline separately and in-depth, rather than merely providing a brief overview over a few months, as is sometimes practiced in certain styles today. The notion that one can attain mastery of a martial art within a few months is, in my opinion, an illusion.

"*Aikidō*, whether we like it or not, derives from *Daitō ryū aikijūjutsu*, with perhaps (very unlikely) the contribution of some techniques from other branches, as the Aikikai seems to assert today in order not to admit its close filiation with *Daitō ryū*."

▶ Luigi Carniel

▶ Morihei Ueshiba at the Omoto-kyo dojo in Ayabe (c. 1920)

Let's Talk About Daito Ryu

"After decades of fog on the official channels of the principal Aikidō associations, Morihei Ueshiba sensei's training background in Daitō-ryū is an accepted and established fact. When Stanley Pranin showed Ueshiba sensei's 1936 Asahi film to Takeda Tokimune, Tokimune sensei's reaction was: 'Yappari sore wa Daitō ryū' [Wow! So he did Daitō-ryū after all!] In your opinion, did Ueshiba sensei content himself with cloning Daitō-ryū, as we have often heard on that side of the fence, or did he transfigure it completely, transcending its original meaning through the influence of Neo-Shintō, as we Aikidō practitioners have come to say?"

"In my humble opinion, both definitions you mention hold some truth. If we turn our attention to the photos of Ueshiba *sensei* in his *dōjō* (cleverly manipulated over the years), where we see the words *'Daitō ryū aikijūjutsu,'* later changed to just *'aikijūjutsu,'* we can already discern a desire to distinguish himself from *Daitō ryū*. Additionally, upon comparing certain footage of Morihei Ueshiba *sensei* from that period with similar footage of *Daitō ryū*, differences emerge. There is a perceptible softening of techniques in

Ueshiba sensei, whereas *Daitō ryū* footage exhibits a warlike rigidity. Furthermore, the working distance of the techniques is not the same.

"Then, the softening of techniques, the physical condition of his son Kisshomaru, according to Minoru Mochizuki *sensei* himself, and certainly the influence of Neo-Shintoism, all contributed to the *Aikidō* of today. Alas, I do not possess the ability to penetrate the secrets of the gods, I can only give my opinion based on my observations and experience. In any case, *Aikidō* today is something new, which has nothing to do with martial arts as I see it."

"Today, observing the world of Daitō-ryū Aiki-jujutsu, one notices a variety of didactics and styles. You have always stressed that what you teach is a side branch of this old school. What do you think are the particularities of the Aiki-jujutsu you teach compared to other styles, such as those of the central branch (dating back to the teaching of Tokimune Takeda sensei), centred on the Mokuroku system with its 118 basic techniques?"

"One should strive to place everything in its historical context and interpret history through the perspectives of those who lived at that time. Former pupils of Morihei Ueshiba *sensei*, who later engaged with Tokimune Takeda, such as Minoru Mochizuki *sensei*, continued practicing the traditional methods taught by their master. Even then, they occasionally referred to it as *Aikidō*, though it fundamentally remained *Aikijūjutsu*. It was only later, during the transformative phase led by Ueshiba *sensei*, that many chose not to follow him in this direction. Instead, they opted to persist with the *Aikijūjutsu* they had previously learned and for which they had received their diplomas. In essence, their divergence was not so much

▶ *Tokimune Takeda*

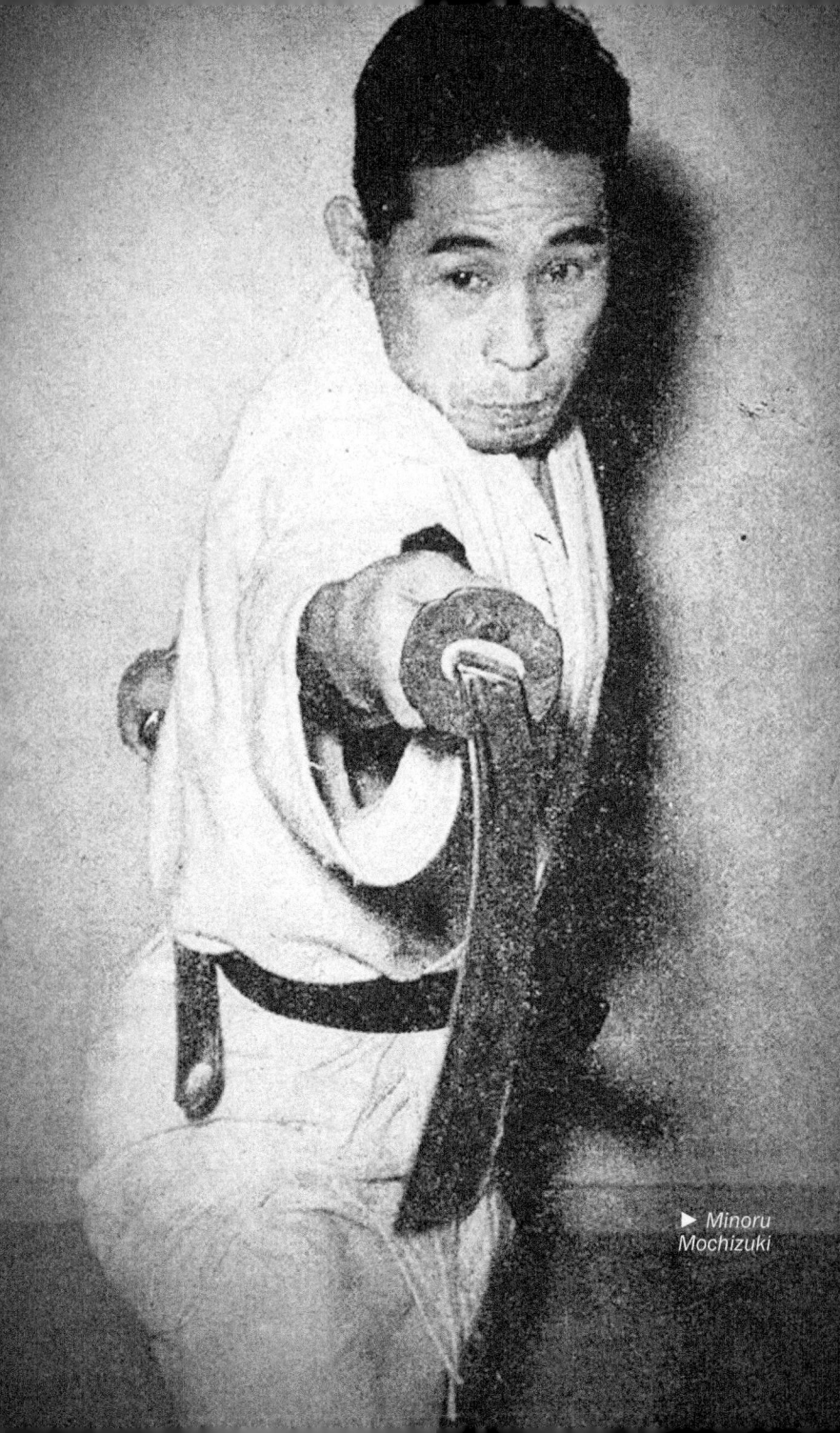

▶ Minoru Mochizuki

from their master but rather from the evolving reality in which what we now recognise as *Aikidō* was taking shape, ultimately becoming a *Gendai Budō*.

"Mochizuki *sensei's* instruction primarily centred on effectiveness. Formed by his wartime encounters and his experiences in France, he came to understand that the practical application of techniques in urban or wartime situations differed significantly from mere training on the *tatami*. One of his key principles was: *'Train as much as you can, for if you falter in a real confrontation, it indicates there is still work to be done.'*

"We are, therefore, distant from what is commonly witnessed in contemporary demonstrations, where attacks are predetermined and choreographed. In the *embukai* (public demonstrations) I participated in during my tenure in Shizuoka, there was no prior preparation. Participants were thrust into the centre of the *tatami*, and attacks came spontaneously, leaving it to each individual to draw upon their instinctive responses. Admittedly, our demonstrations might not have been visually appealing or choreographically refined, but they embodied genuine effectiveness and realism.

"Personally, I've acquired knowledge of around 50 techniques; I'm uncertain if there are more, but the prospect is intriguing. However, when considering the multitude of techniques applied across various attacks and the three distances inherent in *Aikijūjutsu*, along with the variations of each technique, the count roughly reaches this figure. Importantly, despite the diversity, the fundamental purpose and mechanics of each technique remain consistent.

Mochizuki Sensei was a practical man who, in order to facilitate the internalisation of various techniques, devised an innovative approach to practice. Within the *shodan* program, there are just five fundamental techniques categorised by distances: *Tō-ma, Uchi-ma, Chika-ma*. Each of these initial techniques, once internalised, allow, by virtue of certain similarities in the beginning of the form itself or by analogies of certain movements, to later develop the study of further, more advanced techniques with less difficulty for the student.

"This approach sets us apart from the traditional (or current) method, where the instructor randomly selects one or more techniques from the entire school program during each lesson, lacking any clear didactic coherence between them. Thus, at each training session, the technique shown will be new to the neophyte, while, in reality, the underlying principles leading to the movement's goal are comparable to previously learned techniques. Now, to think wrong is a sin, but often by doing that one gets it right: the above way of teaching allows the teacher to maintain a much higher level of knowledge than his students, avoiding the risk of seeing them leave once they perceive they have seen the whole programme.

"Mochizuki sensei, even without ever expressing it too publicly, saw well that even the different branches of *Daitō ryū* had frozen into a stereotyped form that no longer had anything to do with reality. The inclination towards this method may stem from a Japanese approach to transmission or a resistance to change, possibly driven by a desire to uphold a specific attitude that glorifies the stylistic form of each technique. In any case, as Mochizuki sensei expressed it, according to him they would all be dead samurai."

"Many Daitō Ryū teachers claim that this style is characterised by thousands of techniques. What do you think of these hyperbolic numbers?"

▶ Luigi Carniel

▶ Luigi Carniel
and Roberto Granati

"Let's approach this with a dose of reality! Is there genuinely anyone who believes they can master thousands of techniques? A lifetime seems insufficient for such a task. Even with the inclusion of every conceivable variation in the *Daitō Ryū*, considering every distance and type of attack, the sheer number remains unrealistic. It's worth questioning whether the masters making such claims possess an exceptional ability to remember and retain this vast amount of information. Let's stay grounded in our expectations!

"It's easy to overlook that a martial arts school imparts the fundamental techniques for combat, offering a structured form for practical application. The responsibility then falls on the student to customise and adjust these techniques based on the specific situation they encounter. Perhaps this is why some believe there are numerous techniques – a simple move like *kote-gaeshi*, when applied in various circumstances and against different types of attacks, introduces enough variables to create the illusion of endless possibilities. However, at its core, mechanically, it remains a *kote-gaeshi*."

▶ Luigi Carniel

Seifukai's Philosophy

"In one of your articles from a few years ago you state the following: 'After many years of practice and teaching, I have become aware of the metamorphosis - even the change - of Japanese Budō, both in Japan itself, but especially abroad, in Europe and the Western world in general. In a very insidious way, I saw the emergence of what is now called 'Gendai budō', i.e. new martial arts created from scratch from a partial or total knowledge of different fighting arts. These novelties are presented as a legacy of the old Budō of historical origin (...).' Could you explain and motivate the above in more detail? How did these considerations lead you to found the Kōryū Budō Seifukai Renmei?"

"Throughout my journey as a *budōka*, I've had the privilege of encountering a diverse array of individuals – some truly remarkable, and, well, let's just say, others less so. Let's begin with the extraordinary ones – those who have led fulfilling lives immersed in the practice and study of old martial arts. They've not only made these arts accessible to their students but have also instilled a genuine passion and dedication to the practice, carrying forward the legacy passed down through generations of warriors.

"Among those I've had the honor to know personally are

luminaries such as Minoru Mochizuki *sensei*, his son Hiroo Mochizuki *sensei* (in his earlier stages), Yoshio Sugino *sensei*, Kotoken Kajihara *sensei*, Goro Hatakeyama *sensei*, Teruo Sano *sensei*, and the esteemed Madame Toreigai *sensei*, affectionately known as 'Madame Naginata'. These individuals have not only cultivated in me an appreciation for *Kōryū*, the 'old martial arts', but have also instilled the awareness that we are part of a continuum, responsible as custodians for transmitting this old knowledge to the next generation.

"Certainly, across generations, there may be subtle, often unintentional changes influenced by the evolving eras. However, at its core, the practice of technique endures, and its purpose remains steadfast – a warrior's *savoir-faire* proven over centuries. I recognise that this perspective might come across as pretentious, but out of respect for the *sensei* who have guided me, it is my duty to stay true to the path they've laid out, free from pretence or false modesty.

"Regrettably, I must also address the other aspect–a cast of characters ranging from colourful personalities to shameless, audacious, and dishonest individuals. I'd categorise them into two groups: those with some knowledge and those who merely possess it in words. For the former, those who sought to distinguish themselves from the traditional *Kōryū* by creating *Gendai Budō*, I can comprehend the motivation, though I may not necessarily agree with it. The desire to forge one's martial art is undoubtedly strong, driven by a significant dose of narcissism. What could be more gratifying to these individuals' self-esteem than the emergence of a new martial art, touted as accessible to all and falsely proclaimed as the Holy Grail of martial arts? Many teachers have found themselves tempted by this path, a phase of personal self-gratification that, at some point in their lives, consumes them entirely!

"However, it's the second category, those I categorise as

▶ Luigi Carniel

▶ Luigi Carniel

the 'repositories of knowledge within,' that I find most perilous for the reputation of *Budō*. They bring to mind the hucksters at fairs who loudly proclaim, "This way, ladies and gentlemen! This is the invincible martial art. Maximum effectiveness without any effort.' The danger lies in selling illusions to sincere individuals who place their trust in them, unable to discern the truth due to their lack of previous experience. To make matters worse, these individuals often audaciously claim an ancient, obscure historical past for their pseudo-school.

"For this reason, and driven by a commitment to prevent the extinction of old forms of *Budō*, I made the decision a decade ago, along with my son Laurent and Mr. Roberto Granati, to establish a European association dedicated to preserving the old schools (*Kōryū*), thereby honouring the wishes of Minoru Mochizuki *sensei*. While we acknowledge that we are but a modest defense against the influx of new pseudo martial arts, what provides reassurance is that these innovations are transient; they are merely passing trends. The crux is to maintain a resounding and unwavering voice that emphasises the existence and endurance of *Kōryū*. I am cognisant of the challenges that lie ahead, yet concurrently, there is optimism because we are not alone in this endeavour. Many others share in this ongoing struggle.

"Indeed, it is a battle against superficiality, incompetence, and, above all, dishonesty. Our organisation fully understands the formidable challenge ahead, but we persist in our mission to preserve old *Budō*, which otherwise face the risk of fading into oblivion. This is why I employ terms like 'fight' – we are genuinely engaged in a fierce and unyielding effort to sustain the memory and legacy of the ancient masters to whom we owe so much."

▶ Luigi Carniel

The Value
of Reishiki Today

"In a society that is increasingly freeing itself from all forms of ritualisation and where the past struggles to move beyond yesterday, what value remains to be attributed to reishiki in martial arts?"

"*Reishiki* should hold a pivotal role in the study and practice of *Budō*. Unfortunately, we've reached a point where this aspect of martial training is often hastily executed or entirely neglected in many *dōjō*. But what exactly is *reishiki*? It's a ceremonial ritual that marks the commencement and conclusion of an action, whether carried out individually or collectively, as observed in *dōjō* dedicated to *Kōryū* practices. This 'label' gains even greater significance in the context of an art of war. A parallel can be drawn with the modern military, where each day begins with the flag-raising and national anthem, and concludes with the lowering of the flag, also accompanied by the national anthem. This ceremony mirrors *reishiki*, serving as a means to foster unity among soldiers and, similarly, on the *tatami*, it acts as a method to cultivate cohesion among students.

"For example, at the *Hombu dōjō* in Shizuoka, *reishiki* was felt in a very 'martial' way, full of emphasis and depth, with Mochizuki *sensei* reciting at the end of each lesson the *Seikun*, an imperial edict by emperor Meiji dating back to 1890, which the students then repeated. This edict is composed of maxims concerning life, morality, compassion and duty to the nation.

"Contemporary society has become markedly individualistic, prioritising rights over duties. This self-centred perspective has eroded any sense of collective social responsibility. Therefore, it should come as no surprise if certain *dōjō* incorporate activities such as playing sports or practicing music, or even more unconventional pursuits. These endeavours align more with the entertainment preferences of the masses and cater to modern sensibilities. Consequently, the shift in martial arts is not surprising. As I frequently emphasise to my students, martial arts transcend being a mere sport or hobby; instead, they constitute a disciplined practice of both the body and mind, undertaken willingly and purposefully.

"In the contemporary context, *reishiki* might appear outdated, out of sync with our modern sensibilities, but traditional martial arts rely on this ritualistic moment. Consider *Muay-thai*, Thai boxing, for instance; despite its adaptation to the present era, it maintains pre and post-fight rituals. The same principle applies to Japanese martial arts. Rituals are ingrained in their origins, alongside traditions. Eliminating them would create a significant moral void because, in facing life's challenges, humans need to draw on the profound and invisible, something beyond themselves. This doesn't entail embracing cheap mysticism; let's leave such esoteric exaggerations to charlatans and self-proclaimed gurus who exploit human naivety and ignorance. Nevertheless, let's recognise the value of etiquette, discipline, and the moral dimension in martial arts.

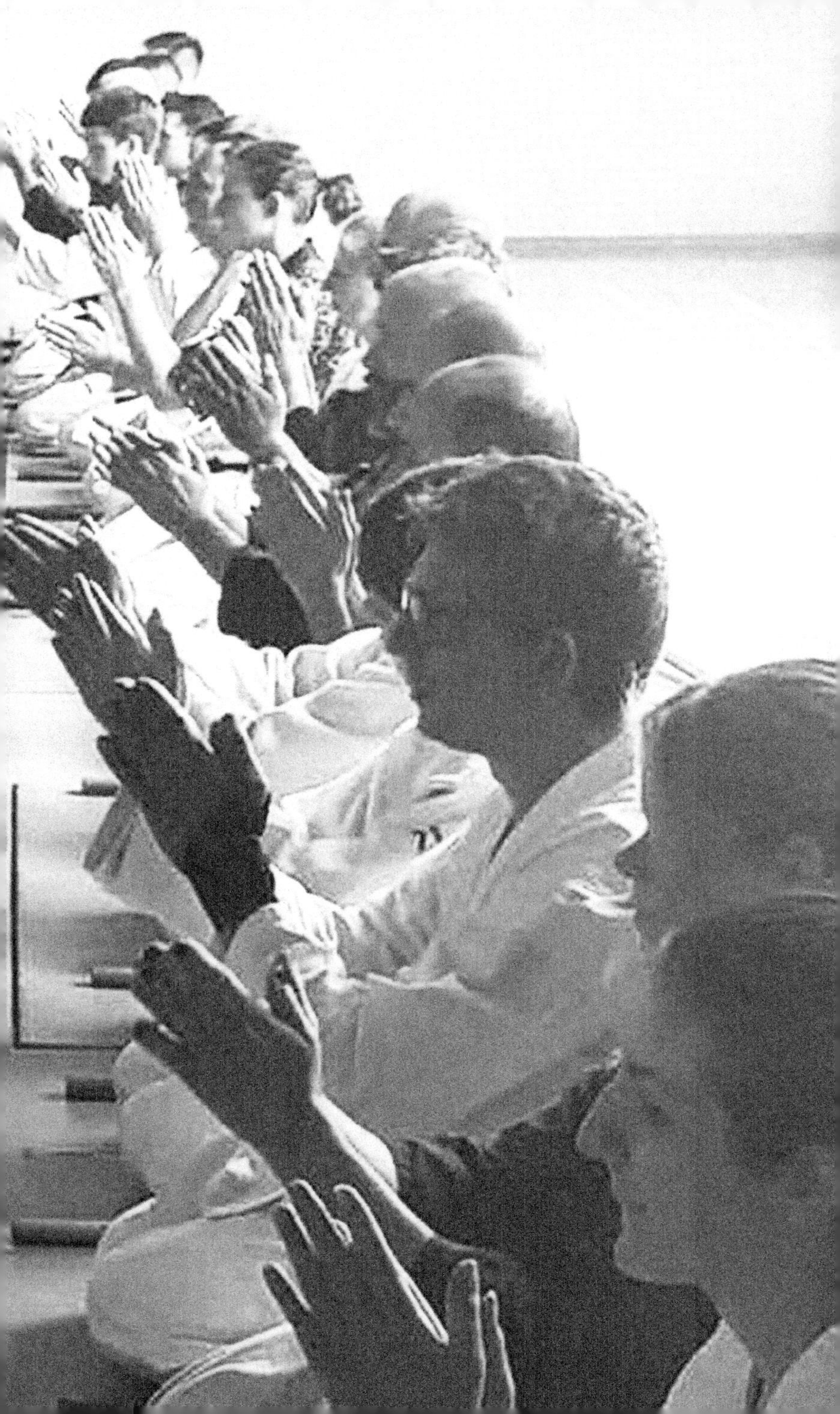

▶ Minoru Mochizuki

Gyokushin Ryu Jujutsu, a Lost Art

"Within the Kōryu Budō Seifukai, you also continue to study Gyokushin Ryū Jūjutsu, one of the schools learnt in his youth by Minoru Mochizuki sensei. Can you tell us more about this type of kōryū?"

"*Gyokushin-ryū Jūjutsu* is an old martial school that has sadly vanished. Minoru Mochizuki *sensei* learned just under twenty techniques of this style from his final representative, Sanjuro Oshima *sensei*. Documents held by the *Kōryū Budō Seifukai* confirm three branches of *Gyokushin-ryū*: *Gyokushin-ryū kenjutsu*, *Gyokushin-ryū ryoto* (the school of the two swords), and *Gyokushin-ryū Jūjutsu*. While *Gyokushin-ryū*, like other schools, encompassed a comprehensive knowledge of the art of war, only the *jūjutsu* branch survived. However, even this branch was not entirely complete, as Minoru Mochizuki sensei lost his master before acquiring the total knowledge of *jūjutsu*. This serves as a tangible illustration of the dynamics contributing to the disappearance of a significant portion of the Japanese *Budō* legacy.

"Terumi Washizu *sensei*, and subsequently, a few other students of Minoru Mochizuki *sensei*, myself included, bear the responsibility of safeguarding what little remains of this school.

"As per Mochizuki *sensei*, the significance of the name *Gyokushin* is tied to possessing a spherical mind, signifying that both technically and mentally, we must avoid rigidity and instead emulate a sphere that, when pushed in any direction, adapts to circumstances. Minoru Mochizuki, while humbly acknowledging that it took him considerable time to grasp the deeper meaning, is the reason we have a partial resurgence of this forgotten art. However, there is a crucial commitment that Mochizuki *sensei* urged us to make: not to blend this art with *Aikijūjutsu*. How should we interpret this commitment today? It doesn't imply a prohibition on studying it during *Aikijūjutsu* lessons, but rather emphasises the necessity to recognise its status as a distinct *Kōryū* and to preserve its independent and distinctive teaching.

"The core principle of *Gyokushin ryū* revolves around the concept of a spherical spirit. What does this mean? A spherical spirit implies a way of life, both on and off the tatami, where all forms of rigidity are rejected, enabling maximum physical and mental adaptability to every conceivable situation. In the art of war, it entails adapting to circumstances, mastering the art of flexibility, avoiding stagnation. Mentally, it emphasises flexibility, comprehension of the essence of words, and proficiency in rhetoric. In my perspective, this embodies the spirit of *Gyokushin ryū*."

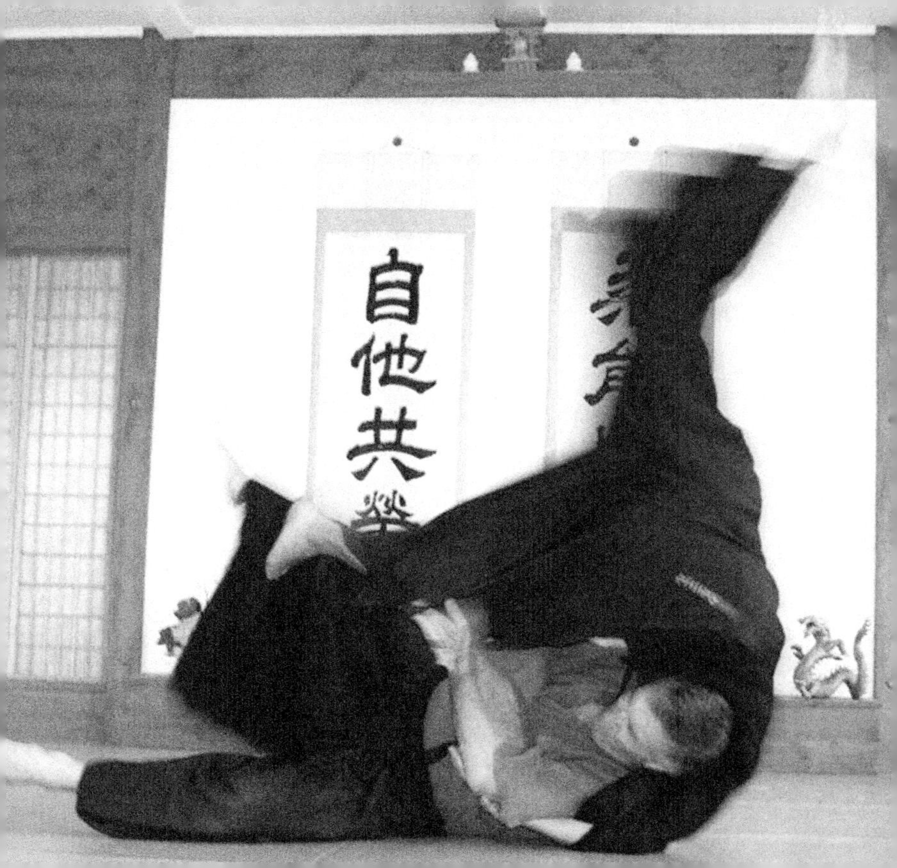
自他共

▶ Luigi Carniel

Forging One's own blade

"From Kajihara Kotoken sensei, your Battodō teacher, you learnt to forge and polish traditional Japanese blades and became a respected tōgishi. What does it mean to be able to make a blade for someone who also knows how to use it?"

"Crafting a *shinken* is an unparalleled joy. It's challenging to convey the mental state one experiences after months of meticulous work with the materials, witnessing the envisioned *shinken* come to life.

"The initial considerations involve the desires of the individual commissioning the blade. These non-negotiable requirements serve as the foundation for contemplating how to proceed, ensuring the ultimate satisfaction of the person for whom the blade is forged.

"As with attaining martial arts knowledge, the ability to craft a *shinken* demands a lifelong dedication. However, the passion to fashion an object like a sword with your hands, intellect, and heart compensates for any encountered difficulties. My practitioner's perspective significantly influences the meticulous attention I pay to details, particularly the blade. It must achieve a delicate balance – sharp yet resilient, with an ideal curve. This involves placing the blade flat on the edge of a surface and gradually moving it away, turning the curve towards the ground as the *monouchi* begins, specifically in the first third starting from the *kissaki*. This detail is paramount for achieving equilibrium when handling the sword, especially in practices like *Iaijutsu*.

"Being a practitioner of the sword art allows you to contemplate details that someone unfamiliar with *Budō* would never consider. For instance, a small detail like the *kurigata* (a small ring through which the *sageo* passes to secure the sword on the belt) needs to be positioned at an adequate distance from the *koiguchi*. This ensures it doesn't impede the hand when gripping the *saya* to execute *battō* (unsheathing action) or *notō* (sheathing action). That, in a nutshell, is the state of mind of a blacksmith who is also a practitioner.

"A few years back, I received the most rewarding recognition for a life dedicated to crafting these magnificent weapons. During the bicentenary celebration of Swiss-Japanese relations, an exhibition showcasing Japanese art was organised at the Ethnographic Museum in Neuchâtel. I was approached with a request to exhibit one of my swords, a proposition I willingly embraced. For the record, I had to reach out to a client to seek permission to showcase their sword, a request they graciously accepted.

"The Swiss Confederation, in collaboration with the Japanese embassy, extended an invitation to the Japanese government for the Crown Prince of Japan to attend the opening ceremony of the exhibition—an invitation that was eventually accepted. On the inaugural day, His Highness, accompanied by all the dignitaries present, graced the event. He initiated a guided tour, displaying a minimum of security, as is the norm in Switzerland. During the tour, he paused in front of my sword, inquiring if it was of Japanese origin. The interpreter conveyed that I was the creator. His Majesty then glanced in my direction, nodding approvingly. In response, I offered a deep bow. I must confess, in all

▶ Luigi Carniel

▶ *Luigi Carniel*

honesty, that my heart was pounding intensely at that moment.

"Subsequently, I learned that an article had been published about me in Japan titled 'The Foreigner Who Does Nihontō.' Today, I can affirm that the current Emperor took a moment to observe one of my sabres.

"I share this incident not just for personal satisfaction, but it's crucial to maintain humility and put the significance of such moments into perspective."

"Do you get more pleasure from forging a katana, or from holding it in your hands during a kata?"

"They are two different pleasures. The pleasure of forging and creating engages you for months, demanding constant concentration, as a small mistake can have undesirable consequences later on. The joy I experience at each stage of crafting the object—emphasising the term 'creation' as it becomes part of one's inner self—is intertwined with the meticulous pursuit of excellence in the final result. Working with the diverse materials that constitute a *katana* requires constant adaptation of one's skills. Forging and polishing focus on the steel, the mechanical aspects of the blade. The *koshirae*, or 'mounting,' involves wood, lacquer, ray skin surrounding the handle, the lacing of the *ito-maki*, and, of course, the *menuki*, *fuchi*, and *kashira*. All these carefully selected elements contribute to the visual delight of the creation itself. Yet, the paramount element is the blade, which must embody solidity, balance, lightness, and sharpness. The fulfilment of these criteria fills me with profound happiness.

"The joy of wielding an authentic *katana* goes beyond the act of creation. It stems from feeling the balance, the rigidity (some blades vibrate), the handle seamlessly fitting into the hand, and an overall sense of lightness. Indeed, during the cutting motion, there's an unusual sensation as if the blade isn't present at all—an intriguing feeling that brings pleasure when working with a sword.

▶ Minoru Mochizuki and Luigi Carniel

The Oxymoron Iconoclast / Transmitter of Tradition

"You often describe yourself as an 'iconoclast', a characteristic I believe was also a prerogative of your teacher, Minoru Mochizuki sensei. What does this adjective mean to you, and how do you reconcile your great respect for tradition with a term that can sometimes be considered an oxymoron when talking about the transmission of ancient customs?"

"Minoru Mochizuki sensei liked to repeat this: *'Beliefs and truths in Budō must not become religious, otherwise they will cause conflict.'* I admit, for that reason, that I am an iconoclast, and I am an iconoclast to myself above all. What does it mean to be an iconoclast? For me it is above all not giving in to ease. My past as an engineer taught me constant questioning, that what is true today may not be true tomorrow.

"This sentiment is equally applicable to *Budō*, and indeed, it is particularly relevant to *Budō*. In a realm where oversized egos prevail, where appearance often overshadows substance, where everyone claims to possess the ultimate truth, and where certain dubious figures are almost sanctified, being iconoclastic becomes essential. Being iconoclastic doesn't imply disrespecting traditions; rather, it involves safeguarding these marvellous legacies from distortion, preventing their use and modification for personal gain, and ensuring they occupy their rightful place. Primarily, it,s about transmitting an ancestral knowledge that doesn't belong to us but of which we are only temporary custodians—a mere link in the chain connecting a warrior past to the future.

"As an iconoclast, I do not position myself as a purveyor of moral lessons. Far from suggesting such a role, I am someone who strives to grant martial arts their rightful place as contemporary instruments of education. This aligns with Minoru Mochizuki *sensei*'s vision, who conveyed that in our country, churches exist to instil morality, while in Japan, this responsibility falls upon the *dōjō*.

"I am aware that my remarks might unsettle some readers because it is often more comforting to adhere to beliefs, even if they are erroneous, than to engage in self-reflection. However, in my view, it is the ongoing process of self-questioning that propels us forward and facilitates improvement. As a blacksmith, I aspire to perfection in my creations, understanding that it is inherently unattainable. Yet, this relentless pursuit enables me to consistently enhance the details, contributing to the continuous improvement of my work.

"The role I've embraced in teaching *Budō* is undeniably challenging, particularly in the manner in which I approach it. To be an iconoclast in this context means challenging established ideas treated as dogma and being critical, even when pinpointing weaknesses. It's acknowledged that nobody enjoys being scrutinised or judged, but criticism should always be constructive and not offensive. In this sense, the iconoclast stands against the stupidity and dishonesty prevalent in the world of Budō, recognising, unfortunately, that this realm is not immune to such issues."

"In Italy, where you have numerous dōjō and students, there are individuals who have criticised you, at times regarding the

▶ Luigi Carniel

► *Luigi Carniel*

nomenclature linked to Aikijūjutsu or Daitō ryū aikijūjutsu. Additionally, there has been controversy over your consistent teaching of Katori Shintō ryū, with some asserting that it might overshadow other dōjō in this discipline. What do you believe is the cause of this dispute, and how do you respond to those who disparage your decades-long efforts that have garnered you numerous students?"

"As I frequently say in such situations: *'the dogs bark and the caravan passes.'* The initial part of the question revolves around the nomenclature of a school or style. However, these critics seem to be more 'realist than king,' revealing their lack of understanding of the Japanese martial world.

"First of all, for Mochizuki *sensei*, the specific labelling of his practice, be it *Aikidō, Aikijūjutsu,* or *Daitō ryū*, was not a significant concern. In the Japanese martial context, there exists a common language and a more technical one when precision is required. While it's true that some individuals, feeling threatened, tend to defend themselves through attacks and controversies, employing fallacious and trivial reasons is counterproductive. If what they teach is credible and students genuinely believe that the instruction aligns with the school's principles, where is the problem? It's often their amateurism or lack of competence that prompts a defensive stance, as they fear confrontations that may expose their weaknesses.

"Regarding *Katori Shintō Ryū*, my interpretation of the practice and understanding of the art might be unsettling, not only in Italy but also among the Japanese. The reason behind this unease, in my opinion, lies in the belief that transmission goes beyond technique and orthodoxy—it encompasses something equally crucial, the spirit that animates this art, martiality in its most profound sense. However, this aspect is often overshadowed. Presently, the focus is primarily on minor corrections, elevated into seemingly crucial details, eagerly embraced by students who flock to witness the Japanese instructor in action. Yet, correcting such minor details alone does not capture the essence of *Katori Shintō Ryū*.

"One might question my authority to make such remarks, and I make no claims to possess absolute truth. These reflections stem from personal observation and research. After decades of dedicated work, I sensed something missing—a dissatisfaction in practice that even the Japanese teachings couldn't resolve. Perhaps Yoshio Sugino *sensei* could have clarified it for me, but in my youth, I blindly followed instructions. Over the years, this feeling of emptiness persisted without a clear identification of its causes. Upon parting ways with Yukihiro Sugino *sensei* (although, crucially, not from Sugino Dōjō as its parent entity), I finally gained the freedom to think independently. It was then that I discovered what was lacking: 'martiality.'

"In terms of controversies, I've consistently faced criticism for my candidness. My intention has never been to harm anyone, but perhaps, owing to my inclination towards moderation and respect, some may have misunderstood these traits as weaknesses and sought to exploit them. In every situation, even in the most intense confrontations, there exists a way to express opinions and engage in arguments. Many teachers who have attacked me were met with a reciprocal response. I encountered particularly insidious controversies when I questioned certain individuals who, out of their apparent incompetence, opted to complain about my perceived actions, which, in their view, undermined the discipline of their school. This is the essence of being iconoclastic—having the courage to hold one's opinions and not accepting everything, even when it comes from the Japanese instructors."

"The term Sogo Budō, meaning the complete and total study of martial arts, is widely used by many teachers today, both Western and Japanese. Diplomas in Sogo Budō are also

► *Yoshio Sugino
e Luigi Carniel*

► Luigi Carniel

frequently conferred. Minoru Mochizuki Sensei believed in the natural ability of an experienced practitioner to instinctively apply all their scholastic knowledge in actual combat. However, based on your account, at the Yoseikan Hombu Dōjō, these aspects were taught strictly separately. In contrast, many contemporary teachers, some of whom studied in Shizuoka like you, integrate this knowledge into their teaching. What is your opinion on this synthesis of martial arts knowledge in modern teaching methods?"

"Once again, the iconoclast perspective comes into play. Following the trend of self-referential *dan* ranks, self-proclaimed titles like *Shihan*, *Soke*, and even *Meijin* (yes, you read that right!), now we have the emergence of titles such as *Sogo Budō* and diplomas claiming the 'total knowledge of martial arts.' What a grand assertion! It becomes even more absurd considering that, in all likelihood, these individuals train only once or twice a week, with sessions lasting at most two hours.

"In the 1970s, a trend emerged where individuals would create new martial arts after claiming to have had a spiritual and esoteric vision, sometimes bordering on the 'miraculous'—such as pool water boiling, celestial voices, or dazzling lights! This served as an optimal way to attract new followers, often perceived as gullible, who blindly followed the mystical figure of the 'sensei guru.' Today, we witness the rise of *Sogo Budō* creators. These are individuals who suggest that obtaining a rank in their pseudo-art equates to having a rank in any style—be it *Karate, Judo, Aikido* or *Aikijujutsu*, Japanese fencing (they often use generic terms as they dare not specifically name a school), and so on. It's disheartening to witness the state of affairs in the world of *Budō*. I'm sure my *sensei* would be dismayed by these developments, to put it frankly.

"Mochizuki Sensei steadfastly avoided mixing martial arts styles throughout his entire life, despite some claims to the contrary toward the end of his life. Sensei dedicated his entire life to the study and research of the secrets of *Budō*. I wholeheartedly align with his perspective on the separate practice of different disciplines. This approach allows the knowledge to interpenetrate each other, fostering a mental and technical structure crucial in real combat scenarios.

"These modern *Sogo Budō* appear to be nothing more than a facade for amusement. I dare to make this assertion because this type of study tends to skim the surface of the discipline without delving into its depths. Following my unfortunate experience with *Yoseikan Budō*, I encountered other instances of *Sogo Budō* and similar syncretisms, all yielding the same outcome: a complete lack of foundation. These foundational elements, crucial in any martial study, were disregarded primarily because they were deemed as a pointless waste of time.

"I could have easily synthesised my knowledge by inventing a new martial art, a path that might have been easier and more lucrative. However, I am acutely aware that such an endeavour would have meant selling my soul. Moreover, who am I to claim the creation of a new art? The disciplines passed down by the old masters offer an abundance to discover and rediscover. I cannot betray their memory, and my unwavering goal is the transmission of what I have received: *Jita Kyo Ei*.

▶ Luigi Carniel

About Luigi Carniel

Luigi Carniel sensei began studying martial arts at the age of 17 in 1962, practicing Wado Ryu Karate. In 1964, he came into contact with the Aiki domain and, starting in 1967, studied Aikido in Bienne. This led him to go to Japan in 1972 at the renowned Yoseikan in Shizuoka under Minoru Mochizuki sensei. Under his guidance, he started studying Daito Ryu Aikijujutsu, Katori Shinto Ryu, and Gyokushin Ryu jujutsu. At the same time, he continued perfecting Karate with Teruo Sano sensei, 9th dan, at Yoseikan.

During 25 years of continuous travels to Japan, he obtained permission from Minoru Mochizuki sensei to refine Tenshin Shoden Katori Shinto Ryu (the oldest school of traditional weapons, considered a 'national cultural asset of Japan') directly at Sugino Yoshio Sensei's hombu dojo in Kawasaki. During his stays in Japan, he also began studying Batto-Do of the Kotoken Ryu school under the direct guidance of Kajihara Kotoken, who initiated him into the secrets of Tameshi Giri.

Thanks to Kajihara sensei's intervention, Carniel sensei obtained permission to study the forging and polishing of traditional Japanese blades. This activity made him a renowned forger and cleaner, as well as a restorer, creating

The Iconoclast

unique, precious, and refined pieces admired in numerous exhibitions. Annually, he also leads workshops for the creation of these blades at his medieval forge, a gift from the canton of Neuchâtel to its distinguished citizen.

Carniel sensei's martial experience formed the basis for developing personal defense techniques for security operators, a commitment he has had since 1978. Currently, he directs personal defense courses for the Neuchatel cantonal police and the training of new police officers at the Swiss Police Institute.

His promotion of Japanese martial arts began in 1969 when he founded the Accademiè Neuchateloise des Arts Martiaux Japonais (www.anamj.ch), which over the years, has increasingly taken on the appearance of ancient schools for the training of bushi class in the Edo period, to which the prestigious Yoseikan also referred. Today, at the academy's dojo in Neuchâtel, Switzerland, practitioners can engage in traditional non-competitive Wado Ryu Karate and Daito Ryu Seifukai Aikijujutsu, as well as Tenshin Shoden Katori Shinto Ryu on different days and times. The academy regularly hosts Tameshi Giri workshops for the Kotoken Ryu school, all directed by Carniel sensei.

Currently, Luigi Carniel holds a 7th dan in Daito Ryu Aikijujutsu Seifukai, 6th dan in Wado Ryu Karate, 5th dan in Tenshin Shoden Katori Shinto Ryu, and 2nd Dan in Batto-Do Kotoken Ryu. Today, Carniel sensei, besides being the President of the Accademiè and a reference point for many teachers in Europe and around the world, is the President and Technical Director of the 古流武道正風会 - Traditional Schools of Budo Seifukai.

The Ran Network
https://therannetwork.com

The Aiki Dialogues

1. The Phenomenologist - Interview with Ellis Amdur
2. The Translator - Interview with Christopher Li
3. The Wrestler - Interview with Rionne "Fujiwara" McAvoy
4. The Traveler - "Find Your Way" - Interview with William T. Gillespie
5. Inryoku - "The Attractive Force" - Interview with Gérard Blaize
6. The Philosopher - Interview with André Cognard
7. The Hermeticist - Interview with Paolo N. Corallini
8. The Heir - Interview with Hiroo Mochizuki
9. The Parent - Interview with Simone Chierchini
10. The Sensei - About Yoji Fujimoto
11. The Teacher - Interview with Lia Suzuki
12. The Innovator - Interview with John Bailey
13. The Uchideshi - Interview with Jacques Payet
14. The Bodymind Educator - Interview with Paul Linden
15. The Budo Bum - Interview with Peter Boylan
16. The Iconoclast - Interview with Luigi Carniel

**Simone Chierchini: The Phenomenologist
Interview with Ellis Amdur**
The Aiki Dialogues - N. 1

Ellis Amdur is a renowned martial arts researcher, a teacher in two different surviving Koryū and a former Aikidō enthusiast.
His books on Aikidō and Budō are considered unique in that he uses his own experiences, often hair-raising or outrageous, as illustrations of the principles about which he writes. His opinions are also backed by solid research and boots-on-the-ground experience.
"The Phenomenologist" is no exception to that.

Simone Chierchini: The Translator - Interview with Christopher Li
The Aiki Dialogues - N. 2

Christopher Li is an instructor at the Aikido Sangenkai, a non-profit Aikidō group in Honolulu, Hawaii, on the island of Oahu. He has been training in traditional and modern Japanese martial arts since 1981, with more than twelve years of training while living in Japan. Chris calls himself a "hobbyist with a specialty", however, thanks to his research and writing he has made an important contribution to the understanding of modern Aikidō. His views on Aikidō, its history and future development are unconventional and often "politically incorrect" but he's not afraid to share them. This is not a book for those unwilling to discuss the official narrative of our art and its people.

Simone Chierchini: The Wrestler - Interview with Rionne McAvoy
The Aiki Dialogues - N. 3

From Taekwondo wonder kid to Karate State Champion, from Hiroshi Tada Sensei's Gessoji Dojo to the Aikikai Hombu Dojo and Yoshiaki Yokota sensei, Rionne "Fujiwara" McAvoy, a star in the toughest professional wrestling league in the world, Japan, has never been one for finding the easy way out. In "The Wrestler", Rionne McAvoy tells his story in martial arts and explains his strong views on Aikido, physical training and cross-training and reveals where he wants to go with his Aikido.

Simone Chierchini: The Traveler - Find Your Way
Interview with William T. Gillespie
The Aiki Dialogues - N. 4

William T. Gillespie, the author of the book "Aikido in Japan and The Way Less Traveled", is a pioneer of Aikido in China. As the sign in his first Aikido Dojo in Los Angeles read, "Not even a million dollars can buy back one minute of your life". This is why W.T. Gillespie resigned from a professional career as a trial attorney in Los Angeles, to move to Tokyo to devote himself to intensively study Aikido at the Aikikai World Headquarters. Currently a 6th Dan Aikikai, his martial arts adventures in Japan and beyond to South East Asia, Korea and even The People's Republic of China became a fantastic journey of self-discovery and personal development that continues to unfold.

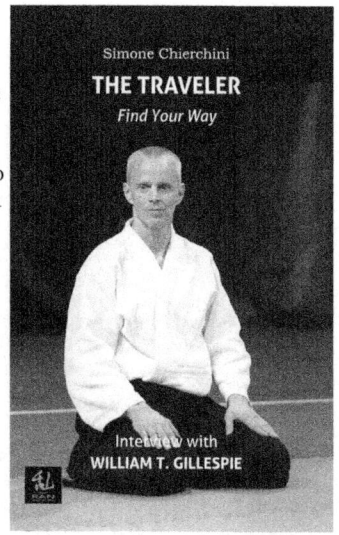

Simone Chierchini: Inryoku
The Attractive Force
Interview with Gérard Blaize
The Aiki Dialogues - N. 5

Gérard Blaize, the first non-Japanese Aikido expert to receive the rank of 7th dan Aikikai, spent five and a half years in Japan where he studied Aikido at the Hombu Dōjō in Tōkyō. In 1975, he met Michio Hikitsuchi, one of the most respected personal students of the founder of Aikido Morihei Ueshiba, and followed his sole guidance until his teacher's death in 2004. Hikitsuchi Sensei was a Shinto priest as well as a high ranked martial artist; in 1969 he was personally awarded the 10th Dan rank by O-sensei. Gérard Blaize has inherited and is still carrying the legacy of Hikitsuchi's holistic Aikido to this day.

Simone Chierchini: The Philosopher
Interview with André Cognard
The Aiki Dialogues - N. 6

André Cognard is one of the most authoritative voices in contemporary international Budo. Born in 1954 in France, he approached the world of martial arts at a very young age, dedicating himself to the intensive practice of various traditional Japanese disciplines. In 1973 he met Hirokazu Kobayashi sensei, a direct disciple of O-sensei Morihei Ueshiba. He received the rank of 8th Dan and on the death of his mentor inherited the leadership of the academy Kokusai Aikido Kenshukai Kobayashi Hirokazu Ryu.

An "itinerant" teacher, a profound connoisseur of Japan and its traditions, André Cognard brings worldwide a technique – the Aikido of his Master; a human message – Aikido at the service of all; a spiritual message – Aikido which, like Man, reconnects with itself when it simply becomes Art.

**Simone Chierchini: The Hermeticist
Interview with Paolo N. Corallini**
The Aiki Dialogues - N. 7

Paolo N. Corallini has been practicing the Art of Aikido since 1969 and during his career he has held numerous positions in this art at national and international level. Author of many conferences on Aikido and its Spirituality, he has written 6 volumes on this martial art. A scholar of Eastern philosophies and religions such as Taoism, Shintoism, Esoteric Buddhism and Sufism, he loves the world of chivalric tradition in general and the Knights Templar in particular. In "The Hermeticist" Corallini sensei brings the reader from Iwama and his meeting with Morihiro Saito sensei to the complex interweaving between the different pedagogies in Aikido; from his memories of the man Morihiro Saito to the future of Aikido and much much more.

**Adriano Amari: The Heir
Interview with Hiroo Mochizuki**
The Aiki Dialogues - N. 8

Hiroo Mochizuki is the heir of a samurai family. Creator of Yoseikan Budo, he is a world-renowned expert in Japanese martial arts.
Son of the famous teacher Minoru Mochizuki, who is considered a Japanese national treasure and was also a direct student of Jigoro Kano and Morihei Ueshiba, the successor of a line of samurai, Hiroo Mochizuki was inspired by his forefathers combative spirit to create Yoseikan Budo.
He adapted the philosophy, pedagogy and traditional practice of martial arts to a new modern environment, as well as to contemporary combat techniques. Besides practicing Mixed Martial Arts before people knew what MMA was, Hiroo Mochizuki has one of the most impressive records in the martial world.

Marco Rubatto: The Parent
Interview with Simone Chierchini
The Aiki Dialogues - N. 9

Simone Chierchini did not choose Budo, he "was there". For 50 years at the forefront and in an enviable position in the Aikido community, he had the opportunity to witness first-hand the major events that have accompanied the birth and development of Aikido in Italy and Europe. Simone began practicing Aikido at the age of eight and has travelled the world as a student and teacher of the art, changing friends, students and occupations but never forgetting to pack his sword, pen and camera. A direct pupil of Hideki Hosokawa and Yoji Fujimoto, Simone has recently founded Aikido Italia Network Publishing, the publishing house specialised in the dissemination of Aikidō and martial arts culture that hosts this interview.

Simone Chierchini: The Sensei
About Yoji Fujimoto
The Aiki Dialogues - N. 10

This publication endeavours to accomplish a very difficult task: that of bringing to life once again the voice and works of one of the most beloved figures of International Aikidō. Yoji Fujimoto sensei has been gone for nearly 10 years and has left behind thousands of students who have who have never stopped mourning him. Since 1971, the year of his arrival in Italy, Fujimoto sensei has dedicated his whole life and all his energy to the practice of Aikidō.
In this book, some of Fujimoto sensei's senior students have tried, within the limits of their abilities and their memories, to evoke the figure and teaching of Fujimoto sensei.

**Simone Chierchini: The Teacher
Interview with Lia Suzuki**
The Aiki Dialogues - N. 11

Lia Suzuki, founder and director of Aikido Kenkyukai International USA, began her Aikido training in 1982 under William Gleason. She soon moved to Japan to train with Yoshinobu Takeda, one of Seigo Yamaguchi's most accomplished students. She lived in Japan and trained extensively in Aikido from 1987 to 1996. At the urging of Takeda shihan, Lia sensei returned to establish dojos in the USA in 1996. She currently holds the rank of 6th dan Aikikai and travels extensively as a guest instructor, conducting Aikido seminars in dojos around the world. Over the years, Lia sensei has dedicated her training to promoting inclusion in the world of Aikido and increasing the popularity of Aikido among young people.

**Simone Chierchini: The Innovator
Interview with John Bailey**
The Aiki Dialogues - N. 12

John Bailey studied Aikido under Tony Graziano and Tom Walker.
He is a graduate of Executive Security International and has an extensive background in security and investigations, having worked as a bouncer, security officer, bodyguard, undercover operative and tactical instructor. He's a life-long student of violence, the behavioural factors and practical implications of it.
He's presently focused on the navigation of crisis periods, and creating fulfilment through life design.
John has studied Aikido for four decades, the past two of which have been dedicated to exploring better ways to train and to teach the art in a quickly changing world.

**Simone Chierchini:
The Bodymind Educator
Interview with Paul Linden**
The Aiki Dialogues - N. 14

Founder of Being in Movement, Paul Linden, an Aikido teacher based in Columbus, Ohio, is a world leader in embodied training, having been active in the field for 40 years. Paul has been practising and teaching Aikido since 1969 and holds the rank of 6th dan. Author of numerous books and instructional videos on applications of body awareness training, Paul leads seminars around the world. Let's hear from him about his particular vision of what Aikido is and can offer to individuals and society in the future.

The Budo Bum: Interview with Peter Boylan
The Aiki Dialogues #15

Peter Boylan, the well-known 'Budo Bum', has been studying Japanese martial arts for over thirty years. After starting with Kodokan Judo, he moved to Japan, where he lived and studied martial arts for almost seven years, practised Iaido and Jodo, and was certified in two koryu.
In this book-interview Boylan offers many fundamental insights into Budo practice, using the approach that characterises his main work, 'Musings of a Budo Bum': he examines how we approach our practice, what motivates us and where we can work to grow.

Printed in Great Britain
by Amazon